# Over 65:
# Writing for Pleasure
# And Profit!

# Over 65:
# Writing for Pleasure
# And Profit!

by
## Dr. Philip Gordon, PhD

Blue Matrix Publications

Blue Matrix Publications, October 2012

*Over 65: Writing for Pleasure and Profit!*

Copyright © 2012, Dr. Philip Gordon, PhD
All Rights Reserved

Blue Matrix Publications

USA:
2995 Woodside Rd Suite 400, Woodside, CA 94062
France:
2 rue Despaty, Voisines, FR 89260

ISBN: 978-0-9847638-8-7

Book Design: Steven Peterson and David Frith

**www.MDG-Consultants.com**
Printed in the United States of America

*This book is dedicated to Jared,*
*who I haven't met yet.*

*-Dr. Philip Gordon, PhD*

# Table of Contents

# Table of Contents

# *Foreword*

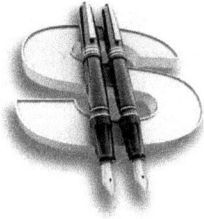

*"The man who makes everything that leads to happiness depends upon himself, and not upon other men, has adopted the very best plan for living happily."*
**-Plato**

## You want to do something significant with the next phase of your life...

Buying this book was your first important step.

Learn to be a successful writer.

Make money writing-even while you are learning.

### *The Over 65: Writing for Pleasure and Profit!* book.

Inside this book you'll find everything you need to get started right away with the *Over 65: Writing for Pleasure and Profit!* process.

While understanding the theories behind the writing craft is essential to becoming a good writer, this *Over 65: Writing for Pleasure and Profit!* book doesn't believe struggling through long, cumbersome textbooks is the way.

We want you to have time to do what's most important for every writer. (Besides, at our age, who wants to waste our time?)

### We want you to have time to write.

That's why the *Over 65: Writing for Pleasure and Profit!* book has been carefully organized into "concise," short chapters, each designed to be read with a comfortable study approach and method.

In addition, each chapter includes thought-provoking insights and **TIPS** that are scattered throughout each chapter to reinforce key concepts, and challenge your understanding of the material covered.

### What kinds of jobs are there for writers "Over 65"?

Whether or not you are over 65 (or near 65) and writing for pleasure or want to write for profit, writing can take you in a variety of directions.

You should always consider your interests and abilities when evaluating a particular type of writing that might be just right for you.

## The *Over 65: Writing for Pleasure and Profit!* book process will show you how to make it happen!

The *Over 65: Writing for Pleasure and Profit!* book will help you with the following:

(1) Are you a self starter, motivated, and self-disciplined?

(2) Do you finish what you start?

(3) Do you refuse to quit?

If you feel uneasy about any of these questions, the *Over 65: Writing for Pleasure and Profit!* book will help build your writing confidence and provide valuable tips on becoming a successful writer.

(4) Do you have a "writer's plan"?

(5) Do you know which markets you want to explore and how you want to approach them?

(6) How much you are going to charge?

Don't have the answers to these difficult questions? The *Over 65: Writing for Pleasure and Profit!* book process will show you how.

(7) Can you stick to a writer's schedule?

(8) Do you have good work habits?

The *Over 65: Writing for Pleasure and Profit!* book will show you the way with advice and guidance.

(9) Do you have a space to write in?

(10) Do you have the right equipment and materials?

(11) What supplies are you going to need?

The *Over 65: Writing for Pleasure and Profit!* book will help you get set-up and provide advice on what you'll need to begin writing.

(12)  Do you like to work independently or with others?

(13)  Do you want to be your own boss?

(14)  How much money do you really want to make?

The *Over 65: Writing for Pleasure and Profit!* book will help you answer these difficult questions and more...

- **All about "Freelance" writing:**

So, you think you're motivated and would like to be your own boss? Make your own hours? Choose your own projects?

The *Over 65: Writing for Pleasure and Profit!* book will show you that "freelancers" have the largest writing market available to seek opportunities for selling their work.

**... and yes, it can indeed be very lucrative!**

## The *Over 65: Writing for Pleasure and Profit!* book process can prepare you for freelance writing markets in:

- **Magazines (consumer, trade and company):**

Opportunities for the nonfiction writer are better than ever. Although the well-written, captivating article is certain to sell, a few types in particular demand are:

- *The headliner* - the controversial story that makes news, gets talked about, sells copies of the magazine.

- *The personality profile* - always in great demand, people want to know about the person behind the name. The tip here is to make sure your piece is timely and about the right person.

- *The service piece* - the how-to article that helps people perform a task that makes life easier, more efficient, or more profitable. A talented writer can break into the quarterly, literary and small magazine field. These publications generally provide aspiring writers a chance to break into the market. Many top magazine editors continually scan other sources for new writing talent.

- **Newspapers (Syndicated):**

Although the competition is tough, the rewards in the syndicate field are outstanding. In addition, there is a large range of columns on such subjects like astrology and aviation to outdoor, travel and lifestyle features. Distribution and printing costs are typically borne by the publication that picks up the column. The residuals or repeat commissions for the printed work can be quite outstanding!

- **Writing for Business and Industry:**

Consider the next time you brush your teeth, take a look at the toothpaste in your bathroom cabinet. You'll discover that the words written on the box and the container were written by a professional writer. Yes, even the part that says

*"...used every day, can be an effective way to prevent tooth decay."*

For the business writers, the market is open ended. There is a 'growing and constant demand;!

**there frankly just aren't enough writers to keep up with the demand!**

The *Over 65: Writing for Pleasure and Profit!* book process can help you identify and approach the large variety and wide range of markets available for business writers. As you sell more and more of your work, it will only just be the beginning in stimulating your thinking about potential sources of business.

## The *Over 65: Writing for Pleasure and Profit!* book process also helps prepare writers for the following writing markets:

- **Annual Reports:**

We would be the first to admit that it's hard to break into this market, but once you do the pay is very good. Sometimes our writers have started in this area by doing work for nonprofit organizations and then pursuing this field through the communications departments of large corporations.

- **Brochures:**

All sizes of businesses, from one-person "ma and pa shops" to giant corporations need brochures – whether a large brochure that resembles an annual report or a small one color "tri-fold" that fits into a standard envelope.

- **Direct (email) and Mail Campaigns:**

This is becoming an increasingly popular means of generating sales leads and mail orders. Consequently, the market for writers in this field is increasing at an unbelievable rate. The *Over 65: Writing for Pleasure and Profit!* book can show you how to make this a very lucrative writing career option.

Here are just a few other writing job ideas for your consideration:

- **Newspaper Work: (Tabloids)**

Those sensational newspapers that assault you at the supermarket check-out lines are big business and they can provide even the greenest of novice "over 65 writer" with colorful writing skills and opportunity to get published.

- **Writing for Film, Video and TV:**

These markets have to fill at least 18 hours a day with fresh, appealing material. This fact makes these areas the highest paying markets for writers. Producers and production companies are always searching for new show ideas, screenplays and great dialogue writers. These are very lucrative markets!

- **Internet eBLOGS and eJournals and eMagazines:**

It goes without saying that as of this version; the internet has exploded with literally millions of paying freelance opportunities for writers in a variety of subject areas and formats. Many of these can provide very lucrative and ongoing income streams for the writers who know how to approach the editors and publishers... also opportunities are bountiful with Website content, online resource documentation, creative writing, etc.

## From the start, let's get some things straight, you are going to sell 75% of your writing!

## As a beginner writer, you ask?

The problem won't be your writing after you finish reading and completing this book.

Your writing will be acceptable. The problem will be how to approach the editor and how to find the topic that he or she might be interested in.

Should you accept this?

## Aren't Over 65 beginners suppose to suffer? Wrong!

Beginners are suppose to learn-and to begin. We don't see where it is written that you shouldn't be earning a satisfactory return on your investment of time and effort while you learn. And where does it say that you can't be in print regularly from the start?

That's why you bought the *Over 65: Writing for Pleasure and Profit!* book and that's what motivated you to do this in the first place.

## Make money writing-even while you're learning!

## We believe that you should be able to sell at least three out of every first four items you write.

And later, when you are a paid professional, you will be topping that rate all the time. Every one of our readers can do it, assuming literacy and persistence. You will be able to do it if you put in the time and effort to complete this book.

This book is structured such that if you follow our step-by-step method, you will be selling, then writing.

This is a professional, systematic way to being a writer and writing. Your success will come from applying this method.

## The *Over 65: Writing for Pleasure and Profit!* book is based on three simple principles:

- It is easy to sell what you write

- You will be paid for your writing as soon as you find a salable idea and follow the approach in this book.

- The amount of material and money you make is directly proportional to the amount of skill and preparation put into it to have it sell.

Most beginning *Over 65: Writing for Pleasure and Profit!* writers think that publishing success comes from the writing, or, from some higher, creative order.

It goes without saying that literacy, clarity and basic grammar and context in a piece of writing are important.

But let's face it; the best writers out there may never be published. Like riding a bicycle you need to learn how to do it, keep your balance and then you get better, and better.

## Statistics show that writers do less and less writing if they don't sell early and often.

Therefore the emphasis of this *Over 65: Writing for Pleasure and Profit!* book is on selling from the onset!

### WHY WRITE?

Beyond the writing and selling, The *Over 65: Writing for Pleasure and Profit!* book sees this method in terms of realizing some of our very basic hopes and dreams without which our lives would be, nearly pointless.

Central to the dream of many is the hope of leaving something of themselves on earth, a contribution or at least a mark on the pages on history.

Yet few of us are as gifted as Beethoven, Michelangelo or Jefferson. Most of us are of more common talents.

Still, the universe is made of all kinds of stars, some not as large, and written works, in print, paid for and thus validated, have their own level of permanence. Some are even brilliant.

Something of yours in print is a piece of immortality, an extension of you when your earthly time expires. Those words become records of you having creatively been here, something tangible, to be shared with future generations.

This is truly a worthy purpose to write. A worthy dream. So much more than putting money in your pockets and filling paper with words.

The *Over 65: Writing for Pleasure and Profit!* book aims to help make your dream of being in print, for whatever reason, a reality.

## And...

## YOU'LL EARN AS YOU LEARN!

Read what some of our readers already say about the *Over 65: Writing for Pleasure and Profit!* book process:

"I have just received a check for $1600 for two short stories."
> E.G. Harrow
> San Francisco, CA

"Since reading the *Over 65: Writing for Pleasure and Profit!* book 12 months ago, I have earned $1500 in my spare time."
> S.B. Barnes
> San Jose, CA

"I had a successful February, getting work included in three publications and earning $800 in total."
> N.N. Maiden
> Seattle, WA

"It's the first piece of work I've submitted and I can hardly believe my luck! They have offered me $500 for it."
> V. Genzisces
> Los Angeles, CA

## "AM I REALLY QUALIFIED?"

If you want to write, yes. In fact, if you have a serious ambition to write you can gain invaluable help from the *Over 65: Writing for Pleasure and Profit!* book.

### And, what's more, you'll find the whole process enjoyable, too!

Let's go to Chapter One and see how easy it really is...

# *Chapter 1*

## Getting Started:
## Understanding "Low and High"
## Risk Writing

*"Put not your trust in money,*
*but your money in trust."*
**-Oliver Wendell Holmes**

## What you sell in the professional writing world is time.

Every writer in print in paying publications must provide copy at a certain level of competence. If not, the copy won't be purchased.

This chapter of the *Over 65: Writing for Pleasure and Profit!* book will show you what you need to get to that skill level and to be at equal footing with all the other professionals out there.

At that point, you are selling 'time use', as we say here, i.e. how much **saleable material** can you produce in a given amount of time?

Therefore, you do not want to risk writing copy that would not be purchased 50% of the time.

In high risk areas, for example, short stories, your time is poorly spent if you plan to eat from your writing earnings. You must write the entire story and submit it blindly to one editor, then another and so on until one (if any agree to use it).

The wisest short story writer would produce hundreds of stories and flood the editors' desks the minute they are finished, hoping by playing the numbers game that the volume would be enough to scrape a steady financial return.

## From our standpoint, that's pretty risky business – "high risk"!

And if the writing isn't up to publication level, then guess what?

You really are putting yourself out there.

**Hey!...we are talking about your time!**

## Let's look at some numbers here for a second...

If a writer sold one story in five and each story took him 8 hours to complete, that's a 40 hour week. And for this example, let's say he is paid $250 for the story on publication.

The same writer queries a magazine about some nonfiction article. He sends out three queries before an editor gives him the "go ahead." He writes the article and it takes 14 hours total earning $350, paid on acceptance.

The $350 is what a professional can expect to receive, and this is just the middle range. The short story paid an average of $6.25 an hour, after a lot of mailing. The short story might take up to five months to circulate before it sells and then the writer might not be paid for another six months to a year awaiting publication.

The article paid $25 an hour, which the writer received when the piece was accepted (or within 30 days upon acceptance). Even if the editor doesn't accept the piece, the chances are higher that the writer could sell the piece somewhere else.

And the chances of reselling the article, by rewriting are also excellent.

**Which turns that $25 an hour first "sale piece" into $100 an hour after the rewrites or reprints.**

So for now, accept this premise: there are two categories of writing:

**"Low" and "High" risk.**

The focus of this Chapter will be only on the category that will bring you a check in better than three out of four times you write.

*Professionals sell, and then write.*

*Amateurs write, and then try to sell.*

## "Low Risk": The Process:

### Principle:

Write only when you have more than a 50% chance of sale. And once you have sold the piece you can increase your profits by selling reprints and rewrites.

---

**Tip:** *You have a better than 50% chance of a sale when you query (we'll talk about this later) and only write once you have received a positive response ("go ahead") from the editor to your sale. Also, you can increase your market sales by simultaneously submitting the same material.*

---

So, if there is such a thing as "formula" to reach your *Over 65: Writing for Pleasure and Profit!* writing goals, then, that's it!

Let's talk about some definitions…

*Reprints* are when you sell an article to other publications after it has been sold to one publication.

*Rewrites* are essentially the same article, based on the same research, but taken from a different standpoint.

Novices make a lot of mistakes when they write; they write something and then they mail it off.

But true professional writers ask the question:

### Who might read their article?

---

**Tip:** *The **really** savvy professionals turn to "The Writer's Market" (or some other internet sites for publishing markets – see reference site in the resources section), and make a list of likely buyers and then, and only then, submit their copy.*

---

## The biggest mistake novice writers make, is writing and sending their articles out cold.

Just think about it for a second, you are an editor and you have the choice between unsolicited material and query letters written by professionals; which would you put more interest in?

Right! You would read the query letters first and then, when you had time you would get around to the unsolicited stuff, if ever!

So there's the "key" to the process, but if it were that simple this book would end here.

**But nothing that is so promising is that simple.**

We will now present a "assignment"that you start and apply the process of this book (you can do them now or return to it later after you have read the entire *Over 65: Writing for Pleasure and Profit!* book) for you to work through which consider some additional factors that will further enhance your understanding of how to sell 75% of your writing and start you thinking about:

- **The type of writing you want to pursue**

- **The market process**

- **The topic you have selected**

- **The choice of markets**

## "Low and High Risk" Writing:

This "assignment" will start by asking you to tell the difference between "Low" and "High" risk writing.

You will be asked to consider a number of questions based upon the following explanations and definitions:

(Remember the higher the potential sales, the lower the risks.)

## (1) NONFICTION QUERIED SUBMISSIONS:

This writing is done only after you have a "go-ahead" (or authorization) to a query, and you can then rewrite and reprint the piece for more sales.

## (2) NONFICTION SIMULTANEOUS SUBMISSIONS:

This is where you must write and send the work unsolicited. You can send many copies of the same piece at the same time. The sales for this kind of work are lower but you might be able to maintain the same selling percentage.

## (3) NONFICTION UNQUERIED SUBMISSIONS:

This is what most beginners do. Get an idea, write it out and then send it in. This way you might sell 20% of your writing. The difference here is the query.

## (4) PROMOTIONAL MATERIALS/GREETING CARDS:

While your percentage will be low, any writer with a great sense of humor turning out volumes and volumes of this stuff can make a lot of money here.

# (5) SCRIPTS:

This usually requires writing and selling to an agent, hoping that you come up with saleable script. Takes a lot of writing in the beginning, yet the pay range can make it worthwhile.

# (6) FICTION:

---

**Tip:** *Let's face it; selling short stories is becoming a lost art. Your first book printed is most often your fourth to seventh attempt, so the percentage of selling what you actually write is very low. Except for just a few exceptions, the per hour basis is also low when (if) you finally sell.*

---

Given the above determinations, fill in the proper category ("Low" or "high") in the space next to the appropriate type of writing:

(1)  Articles                                                    (examples)
                                                                      (low)
                                                                     (high)

      books                                 _____
      Newspaper                          _____
      Travel                                 _____
      Newspaper                          _____
      Weekly                                 _____
      Religious                              _____
      Regional                               _____
      In-flight Magazines            _____

(2)  Humor                                                      _____
      Other nonfiction markets      _____
      TV/RADIO                            _____
      Movie scripts                       _____
      Stage                                  _____
      Fiction Short Stories           _____
      Poetry                                 _____

Please continue and try to answer the following questions.

When and how is copy submitted? (for the following):

(3) Nonfiction Queried Submissions:

(examples)

| | |
|---|---|
| Queried? | (Yes) |
| To whom? | (Editor) |
| When? | (After "*go-ahead*") |

(4) Nonfiction Simultaneous Submissions:
Queried                     _____
To whom?                 _____
When?                     _____

(5) Promotional Materials/Greeting Cards:   _____
Queried?                 _____
To whom?                 _____
When?                     _____


## Now, on separate sheets of paper (typed-double spaced), please write about the following:

Pick a nonfiction subject that you already can write about. (This will be your personal working example as you proceed through the *Over 65: Writing for Pleasure and Profit!* book).

---

**Tip:** *Choose something you already know about because this will the market you'll approach for your first sale) and without doing much research: (i.e. sports, business, home improvement, merchandise, travel, etc.*

---

But first, put together a notebook/journal full of a collection of images and ideas related to the subject.

Then start writing. What already? Yes! Let's see what you come up with.

---

**Tip:** *Remember that you are trying to develop a theme, create an audience and give your subject purpose. As you write, imagine in your mind, notice the little things the details what people are wearing, the surroundings, the climate... the colors, time of year, etc.*

---

Now get started! No more than 1000 words.

---

**Tip:** *Don't forget the simple structural writing principle: "beginning, middle, end".*

---

This probably would be a good place to mention to begin getting yourself organized, set up a writing space, assemble your tools, notebooks, create a filing and retrieval system for both hard and digital copies. Basic writing tools so that you can spend more time writing and less time looking for stuff.

## Let's see... where did I put that Chapter Two?

# *Chapter 2*

## Understanding the Writing Process and Industry

*"Opportunity is missed by most people because it is dressed in overalls and looks like work."*

**-Thomas Alva Edison**

**There's no real magic to selling and then writing articles or books.**

**The process itself is surprisingly easy!**

The marketing starts long before the sale and determines what you write and how.

It starts with an idea and ends with many sales. This Chapter Two explains that process. The real tip here is why didn't you learn this long before now?

There are two issues to consider in the process that can quickly bring your sales to a level of 75% of all queries sent out:

1.  **If you have a good idea that others would want to read about and,**

2.  **You write at the level of the publication and to the readers in the market areas of writing that you want to appear.**

The actual mechanics of getting into print is just getting from that idea, to the sale, to the resale, and to the reprint.

**There are basically two paths to choose from as far as getting your work printed:**

**(A) For queried submissions and,**

**(B) For direct submissions.**

Both fundamentally begin with an idea and both end with either a sale (or a rejection). The similarity of both paths is that they have the same critical decision point in the process; when the editor reads the piece and says "yes" or "no".

The significant difference is when the editor first looks at the idea. On the queried path that judgment is made before you spend major amounts of your time on the travel, research, and effort on the final composition. With direct submissions, the concept or idea is judged only once: after the piece is completely researched and written.

## Let's take a look at the two paths:

## Path A: Queried Submissions.

For this approach, you prepare a letter to an editor proposing whether he (or she) would consider the idea of an article and/or book about a particular subject you may or may not be interested in writing. Either the editor says:

"No", and you could send the query to another editor, until you find one that says "yes" (you would be hard pressed to run out of editors). But at some point you might want to rethink your idea if this fails to produce any results.

Or, an editor says "yes" to a query, indicating that the piece will be seriously considered, and you move forward to:

Completing the research and writing the piece.

## What kind of writing follows this kind of approach?

Below is a sample nonfiction article (musician/saxophonist: Wayne Shorter personality interview):

### Wayne Shorter: The Man and the Legacy (excerpts)

During our conversation—shared just as he was preparing to put the finishing touches on his ideas for his upcoming show with the SFJAZZ Festival in October—Wayne revealed his sincere feelings towards his life, his music, his friendships and, his respect for the many world class musicians with whom he has collaborated with throughout his impressive career; and we explored his evolution as an artist and these relationships, and his passionate commitment to spirit of the music, life, and his spontaneous, improvisational approach.

**The Over 65 Author:** Your *Footprints Live!* (with Danilo Perez on piano, John Patitucci on Bass, and Brian Blade on drums) is your only live CD and it's all acoustic, can you compare this CD to some of your earlier work with groups such as Weather Report (where you collaborated with Joe Zawinul on material)?

**Wayne Shorter:** The biggest difference to me, was, one was electric and the other was acoustic, one was in a different space and time, and the other was in a current time and space. Weather Report had different personnel at that time and space, with different stories to tell, with a different form and space on the page to tell the story.

**The Over 65 Author:** The compositional process was different between you and Joe on Weather Report, what was the concept with the *Footprints Live!* CD?

**WS:** There's a compositional process on a live performance, the composition meaning...what comes about, once it's done, it's a composed piece. The personnel on *Footprints Live!* mainly were at liberty to extend themselves from where the were formally accustomed to playing with their own groups. They then extended themselves from those kinds of situations to a place where...they didn't have to think about a group or the personalities they were in their own group, (where they were band leaders)... it was a true collaboration.

**The Over 65 Author:** That's right, Danilo, John and Brian all have their own groups)... so when you guys got together, you were more spontaneous with the music?

**WS:** Yes, they didn't have to think about looking for a sound, or looking for a musical signature... they were composing something with the knowledge and feeling they had about the piece.

**The Over 65 Author:** How did you hook-up with Danilo, John and Brian)... how were they chosen?

**WS:** I knew that John lived in New York, he moved from California to New York, and I had heard about Brian Blade for sometime, and I saw Danilo on television the first time with Dizzy Gillespie a while back, and then met him in Washington, D.C. and then, slowly began to hear him (Danilo) perform... like a spot check kind of thing, I wasn't checking him out...but after meeting someone, I kind of...in my mind, initially threw the colors together of how these guys would sound together, I was thinking: 'I think this is going to work'.

## Path B: Direct Submissions,

Below is a sample novel submission (Charles Baudelaire: Life in Paris):

On the 20th of August 1857, Charles-Pierre Baudelaire appeared before the sixth court of the Tribunal de la Seine. The advocate for the prosecution, Ernest Pinard, was one day to be the French Minister of the Interior; but his true claim to fame was that he was chosen to condemn one of the masterworks of French literature: Les Fleurs du Mal. Charles Baudelaire who had stumbled into this courtroom in the midst of a life of dramatic consequences, was already, as his advocate Gustave Chaix d'est-Ange, would state in his defense 'a great artist and a deep and impassioned poet'. Pinard was an established lawyer at thirty-five. Chaix d'est-Ange was only twenty-four.

As so often is the case in history, this court decision, however misconstrued, had a tremendous impact in the world of literature. The judges' verdict, so it seems, exceeded even M. Pinard's hopes. The charge of offending religious morality was set aside. However, six incriminated poems were suppressed, and by order, they were not to be republished. Charles Baudelaire was sentenced to a fine of 300 francs, and his publishers (Malassis and De Broise) a fine of 100 francs apiece for offending public morality.

The condemnation of Les Fleurs du Mal in the late summer of 1857, was for Charles Baudelaire, one of the saddest moments in his life, however, he had been 'condemned, not judged', as Champfleury would write in his defense and the court, even at the time, seemed to understand that it was dealing with the fate of a truly talented genius, and ever since, the worldwide appreciation and interest in his writings and life have only grown.

But the life journey for Charles Baudelaire leading up to this event is a tale of many facets. As Charles Baudelaire was not a poet immune to struggle and confrontation and had dealt with severe blows to his very existence many times before.

Yet, as with so much else about his life, nothing went quite as planned. Baudelaire had squanderer his inherited fortune, lived day-to-day for years confronting his family, health and financial issues, and all the while, would continue to produce volumes of poetry and would become one of the most studied French poets of all time.

Charles Baudelaire is often considered to be one of the greatest poets of the nineteenth century. A revolutionary in his own time, Baudelaire led a cynical, often despairing lifestyle. Today, he is still very well known, not only as a poet, but as a critic as well. Rarely has there been such a radical, yet, brilliant man.

The direct submission path is far easier to follow but in the long run can prove to be more costly and riskier. With this approach, you have to determine the type of readership, prepare an idea, research the idea, write the piece and then send it directly to the editor.

## What kinds of writing are sold by direct submission?

Fiction and short stories, novels, fillers, greeting cards, most newspaper submissions, in-flight magazines and religious material.

Others can be found by researching the internet (or *The Writer's Market*) or by taking a look at individual publications you might want to be published in.

Both approaches lead to a key "moment of truth" - and possible payday.

One is more difficult, and needs to be more calculated. The other is as direct as it can be.

Relative to your bank account, the queried and direct submission paths aren't evaluated on the same basis when an editor gets ready to make a buying decision.

## The slower route in time pays the greater amount than the less lucrative 'express lane.'

If the editor receives a piece from the queried path, he/she knew it was coming.

This approach has the editor involved in the process of its creation and therefore a psychological investment in its success. That connection is in your favor, but only if the queried piece lives up to its promise.

Direct submissions, on the other hand arrive without notice and have to pass the test on the basis of first impressions.

Combining the uncertainty of directly submitted material with the time invested in its full preparation, you can probably see why the queried submission is preferable

The queried approach isn't completed until you the writer are given solid assurance that the finished product will be given full consideration for acceptance and is therefore worth the cost in time and expense.

The only way to even reach near this level of security with the direct submission approach is when many copies of the same piece are sent to different markets at the same time, on the belief that in more markets the prospects of someone buying it would offset the risks for going through all that preparation risk.

## Let's look at the routes in a few markets for the queried approach:

## Articles:

If every "go-ahead" received by you from an editor resulted in a sale, you would literally sell 100% of what you wrote. But that doesn't happen.

Let's assume you provided to editors exactly what you promised in the query what you were going to write about at the outset. It is a fact that only 50% would even actually get purchased! And even if you had a great relationship with the client; the editor, you might be able to get back up to 80% of your output increases and you develop a following with key editors.

But that's not the 75% that we promised you when we began with this book and you started to put this process into practice.

Reprints should more than make up for the difference from the 50%. And that would be from selling the article again to another magazine or publication, with little or no copy changes. With this approach you could quickly boost your average to 100% or more!

---

**Tip:** *The approach here is not that you are relying on these reprints or subsequent submissions, but that you don't have to invest the time and cost in an article until you have the assurance of the initial acceptance.*

---

### Wayne Shorter: The Man and the Legacy
### (excerpts continued)

**The Over 65 Author:** You seem to be using the tenor saxophone more on *Footprints 'Live'* than on the earlier Weather Report material where you were using the soprano. Eight out of the ten tracks were tenor, any reason for that?

**WS:** The tenor can be mixed and heard in an acoustic situation better, from the middle, down, below the iceberg of sound, undertones, overtones, sidetones, perpendicular tones, everything… and it's left up to the mixing job to separate everything.

**The Over 65 Author:** Did you play a number of these tunes just with the soprano to see how they would sound?

**WS:** I thought about the soprano, like when we were playing for about nineteen thousand people in Tokyo three weeks ago, in Tokyo Stadium.

Herbie's Band was there, another group from Norway and a Big Band from Cuba. I used both the soprano and tenor, the group from Norway had all this techno, electric, all kinds of stuff…

**The Over 65 Author:** Did you play an acoustic set to broadcast to that large a crowd?

**WS:** Yes, the other bands had synthesizers and everything, they had their trumpets hooked-up to interface with everything… and Herbie had his Future-to-Future Band, which has allot of electronics… so I used the soprano a lot in that setting, and when we finished we got a standing ovation. And you know it's different in Japan, everybody is historically so polite, they don't even move in their seats normally, so when they stood up… well, that was a great experience.

**The Over 65 Author:** I heard you were playing just after Tokyo at a peace conference, how did that go?

**WS:** The Peace Conference had hundred-piece orchestra, a whole ballet and dance segment, with singer Anita Hall… all in conjunction with promoting world peace… we placed flowers with our families in Arizona… they had four wreaths, for myself, Herbie, Dr. Carter (Dean of the Chapel at Morehouse College), the grand nephew of Alfred Nobel, Michael Nobel. Also there was the grandson of Gandhi, UN representatives, all these beautiful people from all over the world were there.

**The Over 65 Author:** We can look forward to allot of new music coming from all of these inspirational people and experiences?

**WS:** There are more (World Peace) events coming, there is a big orchestra coming from Brazil, that started in the ghetto of Favela, the deepest ghetto in Brazil, allot of those people started playing when they were only seven years old and now they're seventeen.

**The Over 65 Author:** So are you thinking about doing a Latin CD?

**WS:** It won't be just Latin, I just got this orchestras' CD, they're doing music of the world, they are not thought of as a novelty, they are not thinking about the Americanized approach to Latin music, which is to put a clave rhythm to all of these great pieces.

**The Over 65 Author:** You've played with so many world-renowned musicians throughout your career; Maynard Freguson, Art Blakely, Weather Report, Herbie, your own bands, what's been you most memorable 'life' experience so far?

**WS:** That would have to be my experience with Miles Davis. Miles Davis used to say:' I am not what I do, I do what I am'. That's when we musicians would watch musicians on shows like Johnny Carson, and we'd call each other on the telephone and ask: 'Do you think he's going to get to the couch?' you know, beyond the instrument, a human being. Dizzy Gillespie was the first one to make it to the couch. What I'm speaking about is the whole change in philosophy about management, the corporate thing, like record companies… it used to be they didn't want you to do any talking, just wanted you to play. Well, it ain't like that, that's all changed, the artist has to get totally involved and do everything themselves at this point.

## Books:

Nonfiction book sales are harder to calculate, since reprints are not likely. On the other hand, a possible saving step to further time and expense is available.

You would query in the similar fashion to the article approach, and then research and write only when you receive a go-ahead. A positive response would indicate that a contract would be issued upon receipt and approvals of certain number of chapters, usually two or three. This way you would only write this much copy before you would get a financial commitment from the publisher.

Few book editors encourage writers unless the editors are serious about following through, so this go-ahead probably proves this 75% potential selling ratio.

If you as the writer clear this first hurdle – meaning if the first chapters are accepted, the contract is usually drawn up and honored. Later the deal could fall apart, if the writer fails to produce the book or the quality of the subsequent chapters are inferior to the initial chapters or the publishing house goes out of business, etc.

The length of time to write a book, plus human and business irregularities, present more potential pitfalls than articles. This is a safer path to follow for a lot of writers than articles because of the fiscal follow through and the amount of money involved. (Keep in mind the percentage is harder to prove.)

So the question is, for the novice writer:

## What can you write so that you can quickly strike "paydirt" and sell your work?

A true writing professional would ask it another way:

## How do I sell, and then write?

For articles and books the process is virtually the same:

(1)   Idea

(2)   Query

(3)   "Go-ahead"

(4)   Research

(5)   Writing

(6)   Mailing

(7)   Check-cashing

(8)   Rewriting and reprinting

Here's the process in greater detail.

This part of the Chapter Two is important, because it is the basis for your ongoing "assignment" that you are developing:

## The Writing Process:

### Step 1:

In one sentence, what is the subject of the article (or book) you want to write and sell?

### Step 2:

Who might benefit from reading your article? Who would be most interested?

What kind of readers would select your specific subject from a variety of choices?

### Step 3:

Which publications might these readers buy and read?

### Step 4:

Review the broader market that is related to your work, specifically those markets which are similar to or identical to yours.

Therefore you must check the reader's guide to Periodical Literature (now posted on the internet) and specific subject indexes for at least the three previous years, then:

- **List the articles that are closest to your subject.**

- **Cross-check newspaper indexes for the past three years and provide the same information.**

## Step 5:

Have the publications listed in (3) and (4) printed articles within the past three years that are similar to the one you propose?

## Step 6:

After each publication, note the name of the person you should contact (editor, etc.) with the title and address.

Then list the following information:

a.  Does it pay on acceptance or publication?

b.  How much does it pay for work as long as yours?

c.  Does it prefer query or direct submission?

d.  How often does it get published?

e.  What percentage of it is written by freelancers?

f.  What is their preferred piece length?

g.  Is there any other information provided that will affect its placement on your list?

## Step 7:

Now rank your market in its priority order, based on when the buyers pay, how much, frequency of publication and percentage of freelance material used per issue.

## Step 8:

Read the latest issues (or concept issues) of your target publications, front to back. Select the articles that are most similar, in the form not topic, to the piece you will prepare.

Outline each article; write out the lead and conclusion to each by hand. Attempt to identify the publication's readers by age, sex, occupation, income range, education, residence and other pertinent factors.

## Step 9:

Prepare a list of resources for possible information availability if you should proceed with the article:

a.   Similar articles

b.   Card catalogs and books on the subject

c.   List of people to consult for information, quotes, etc. and reasons that they are being contacted.

## Step 10:

From the information that you have gathered on the specific target publication and/or editor and from the research you have done on a particular subject, select the materials you need to write a professional "query letter". (To be discussed in a following chapter.)

## Step 11:

Write a query letter for your target publication.

## Step 12:

If you receive a positive response (and you will if you have done the above steps), plan your article to determine what you still need to finish it.

## Step 13:

Complete the needed research.

## Step 14:

Write the manuscript or article in final draft form. Include on separate paper at least five additional leads.

## Step 15:

Select the best lead, edit the draft, type the final version, keep a copy and mail it (with illustrations?) to the editor who gave you the go ahead.

## For Simultaneous Submissions:

When you prepare your market list (step 3 above), review it to avoid circulation overlap. Then, rather than following the query process, prepare a basic manuscript avoiding specific references, i.e. geographic, that would prevent it from being universal or of long term use. Make copies of the basic work. Where it would enhance the salability, add a personalized cover note or letter. Mail the submissions to the prospective editors.

Before we begin an assignment on the previous material, here's some questions (and some just to think about) on the writing process. Most of this information bears repeating as it is core to the *Over 65: Writing for Pleasure and Profit!* writing process:

## Step 1:

In one sentence, what is the subject of the article (or book) you want to write and sell?

## Step 2:

Who might benefit from reading your article? Who would be most interested?

What kind of readers would select your specific subject from a variety of choices?

Rank all of those potential readers in order, placing those who would derive the most benefit first.

## Step 3:

Which publications might these readers buy and read? Prepare a market list of these publications that are most likely to buy your work.

## Step 4:

Review the broader market that is related to your work, specifically those markets which are similar or identical to yours.

Therefore, you must check:

*Readers Guide to Periodical Literature* and specific subject indexes for at least the three previous years, then:

a.  List the articles that are closest to your subject (make a list on a separate sheet).

b.  Cross-check newspaper indexes for the past three years and provide the same information.

## Step 5:

Have the publications listed in (3) and (4), printed articles within the past three years that are similar to the one you propose?

If so, which ones?

## Step 6:

After each publication, note the name of the person you should contact (editor, etc.) with the title and address.

Then list the following information:

a.   Does it pay on acceptance or publication?

b.   How much does it pay for work as long as yours?

c.   Does it prefer query or direct submission?

d.   How often does it get published?

e.   What percentage of it is written by freelancers?

f.   What is their preferred piece length?

g.   Is there any other information provided that will affect its placement on your list?

## Step 7:

Now rank your market in its priority order, based on when the buyers pay, how much, frequency of publication and percentage of freelance material used per issue.

## Step 8:

Read the latest issues of your target publications, front to back.

Select the articles that are most similar, in the form not topic, to the piece you will prepare.

Outline each article; write out the lead and conclusion to each by hand. Attempt to identify the publication's readers by age, sex, occupation income range, education, residence and other pertinent factors.

## Step 9:

Prepare a list of resources for possible information availability if you should proceed with the article.

(a)   Similar articles

(b)   Card catalogs, websites, and books on the subject

(c)   List of people to consult for information, quotes, etc. and reasons that they are being contacted.

## Step 10:

From the information that you have gathered on the specific target publication or editor and the research you have done on a particular subject, select the material you need to write a professional query letter.

## Step 11:

Write a query letter for your target publication.

## Step 12:

If you receive a positive response and if you have done the above steps you will, plan your article to determine what you need to finish it.

## Step 13:

Complete the needed research.

## Step 14:

Write the manuscript or article in final draft form. Include on separate paper, at least five additional leads.

## Step 15:

Select the best lead; edit the draft, type the final version. Keep a copy, mail it with illustrations to the editor who gave you the go ahead.

**Now, on separate sheets of paper (typed-double spaced), maximum length to be 1500 words.**

Assume that you have been given the "go-ahead" on your first queried subject, using the Chapter One topic as your starting point.

Now we need to see if you can put an "angle" on it, a "spin", or a particular "attitude" to make it more interesting.

So now narrow your subject topic down to one point, (or theme) that could be summarized in one single sentence.

Proceed to use description (the details you developed from Chapter One):

Add narration, movement, structure from beginning to end, and start to think about it in terms of making it interesting to read and informative.

# Chapter 3

## Designing and Selecting a Topic

*"Price is what you pay.*
*Value is what you get."*
**-Warren Buffet**

## Begin by starting with an idea.

## Not just any idea.

As just any idea well written and marketed sufficiently will find a place to be printed- if you don't care where or how much you get paid for all of your time.

But that's not our intent, the goal of the *Over 65: Writing for Pleasure and Profit!* book (Since whom, at our age, has any time to waste?) is to get you into print often and profitably, so you must consider ideas that are easily and widely marketable.

It's really not that hard to do. All you have to do is remember that there are people out there that want to read about themselves, articles and stories similar to their own lives, or what they would like them to be (how they might want to be in fact or fantasy).

That's what you need to write about.

---

**Tip:** *The easiest way to find out what sells is to find out what prospective readers care enough to buy.*

---

## Start with a publication.

There are two ways to match words to prospective readers. The most common approach, at least for most beginners, is to come with an idea and then find the most appropriate market for it. The second way and the *Over 65: Writing for Pleasure and Profit!* approach, is to start with a magazine and then write to that particular audience.

To proceed with the Over 60: Writing for Pleasure and Profit! approach, think of the editors as farmers who plant and disseminate ideas to nurture the mind. If you want to sell your ideas to editors, you would be best to see what kind of seeds they already have been planting in the past, the kinds of ideas that they are used to cultivating and then offer some seeds that will also have a chance to take root in their garden.

First pick a specialized kind of magazine; travel, auto, music, arts and then focus on the top three serving the readership. Go to the library (or on the internet) and see how and where each magazine is indexed.

Next, find the last three or six or twelve issues of each magazine and then do the following:

Prepare a two-column list for each publication. Separate the list into:

(1)   Articles and,

(2)   Departments/columns.

Under each note the subject and the author of every item printed.

See which of the authors listed appear in the masthead. (Next to circulation and address information) That will show you the percentage of material prepared by in-house and that bought by freelancers.

## Review this list.

Topics regularly covered by the department or column aren't likely to be bought from the outside as articles.

Recent articles show that what the readership expects on those pages.

For example, a travel magazine that stresses "seeing the city for $10 a day", "or great restaurants for meals under $5" and "how to pack perishables for camping" isn't directed at jet setters or persons on fixed incomes.

If you plan to write for this magazine, think "low-budget, outdoors and young" with practical, detailed, how-to articles.

Now compare the list from all three magazines.

How do they differ? Is something covered in a column by one appropriate for an article in another?

Mark your observations on the list.

• Are there articles about the same topic in two of the magazines?

• How do the approaches vary?

• What does that tell you about the differences in the readership?

• Where does the index fit in?

Study it so you can get an idea of when and what items are being used. For example, if the October issue has been traditionally dedicated to ski vacations and holiday get away preparations, you know the kinds of ideas that are best suited to be presented at that time.

A close look at rival magazines will tell you where they are heading and how they are traditionally different. It will provide topic constraints beyond which the editors don't tread.

Now make a list of 10 to 15 topics or ideas within the subject range of all three magazines, check to see how each magazine has treated each subject, and try to guess which approaches would mist closely match each publications needs.

This is how to look for ideas and topics from a magazine study.

Find out what an editor wants by studying what they have used. Does this sound like copycat journalism? So what, readers buy magazine to satisfy their curiosities or needs. If you want to be paid to appear in print, you get to satisfy them in new and exciting ways!

---

**Tip:** *Here are a few suggestions that might give you some fast saleable ideas:*

*Holidays—Christmas, New years, St. Patrick's Day, etc. Dates, Anniversaries or Events—That have happened in the past of historical significance or is getting ready to happen in the future.*

*Newspaper Articles—News is facts about topics, today's news is tomorrow's magazine article and a future book it's just had more polishing and more details and don't worry about copyrighting. If you use the facts in an article just double check and make sure they are correct.*

---

The *Over 65: Writing for Pleasure and Profit!* book strongly recommends that you set up right now your "Idea book"

So you need to get organized and not go about a haphazard way of keeping your ideas. (The older we get, it's either we have more to organize, or we have more trouble keeping track of more stuff. I can't remember which…?)

## Hardcover Version:

A three-ring binder with at least 500 pages of paper would be a good place to start, with a spate page for each idea. At three ideas a day, times five days a week would take you days to fill it. Still bankers hours by anyones accounting.

## Digital Version:

Arranging your laptop with digital files according to the following "logic tree":

* Ideas?
  Files A-Z

- Type of Publications?
  List those you are interested in every market?

- Etc.

By the way, there are excellent software programs that do this very same organizing, for example: www.clipnotes.com

Tip: The very act of writing down these ideas and having them organized in a writing file (alphabetically) will do more good in the long run then, the actual ideas themselves.

This idea book becomes an excellent place to compile background information for ideas that are just in the formative stage. Clip and tape articles and bits of information that you find from a variety of sources.

Sometimes what you will find is that you have two ideas that are strong enough and similar enough that they can be merged into other ideas for an even stronger idea.

## "Idea Book" Format (Each Page).

- Date:?
- Idea:?
- Category:?
- Markets:?

The final reasons for the idea book, particularly for the beginner writer is that it forces you to do something every day that reminds you that you are a writer - and you may not even be writing. In a way, it's like forcing yourself to get up every morning and put on your running gear and go out for a run because you call yourself a runner.

And having to come up with three ideas each day will train you to see ideas. This will seem ridiculous after you have been writing for a while. Professionals can think up enough ideas in one hour that can last them a lifetime, but beginners sometimes just have a little trouble taking that first step.

## Mechanics of the "Idea book", both hardcopy and digital.

(1)   Write your ideas in a notebook, one per page.

(2)   As new information becomes available add to the idea page.

(3)   If you write about an idea, conduct a "feasibility" study, you will find new ideas for other articles.

(4)   Prepare a market list which will be part of the feasibility study.

(5)   When you query or submit on a topic, note it on the page as well as the date.

(6)   When you have enough information on an idea you should transfer the information from the idea page to a folder. This usually takes place after the feasibility study and the query has been written.

(7)   Keep your basic idea and research filed by subject. When you receive the "*go ahead*" to a query or sell "simultaneous submission", open a different file under that publications name.

## Is this worth the time and hassle?

## You bet!

Unless of course you are drowning in ideas and fully involved in bringing your ideas to print (also your bank account is flooded with money?).

Today is the day that you go out and buy that three-ring notebook and lots of paper and set up those computer files!

# *Chapter 4*

## Search and
## the Feasibility Study

*"Take calculated risks.
That is quite different than being rash."*
**-General George S. Patton**

Simply stated, the feasibility study for queried articles is the result of getting a positive response from defining and selecting a topic, outlined in Chapter Three and choosing an appropriate idea or topic to write about.

## The purpose behind the feasibility study is straight forward enough:

*Is it feasible to expect to be paid a reasonable price for an article about this topic?*

*And,*

*Is it actually feasible to write an article about what you promised in your query letter to the editor?*

You might ask: When do you do the feasibility study? Good question.

The feasibility study is done to reduce the potential time spent and to increase your selling ratio or percentage.

From a marketing standpoint, the feasibility study is done to determine who would want to read about your topic, what publications they read, when and how much those specific publications pay for articles, which have used similar articles in the past and based on this information you should then be able to put together a marketing list – in order, as to how you go about your query efforts.

From a writing perspective, you want to know more about the articles in print about your topic: anecdotes, quotes and other information as well as the sources for each.

As you look at the market list you will be able to tell whether the subject is worth investigating and spending more of your time to produce the copy.

Further analysis of the research will tell you what to promise in the query so you know what you can actually deliver if and when you receive the "go-ahead" from the editor.

**Tip:** *Spend the least amount of time at the feasibility stage to focus on the largest amount of relevant material. The goal would be to then write a query letter then shouts with confidence and wisdom.*

In the beginning, for novice writers, the feasibility study process takes a lot of time. But as the process comes more familiar the amount of time required is less.

What you don't want to do is start a feasibility study before you, the writer, know whether a topic will result in a sale. And to proceed with the query letter that carries no guarantee of compensation, is a financial risk.

Properly approached, you can reduce the risk involved in doing feasibility studies and eventually turn topic after topic into reliable steady income.

But you must persevere and follow the feasibility guidelines:

## MARKET FEASIBILITY STUDY GUIDELINES

### Find your Readers and assume that you have a topic to write about.

Your first step would be to find the magazine who would buy what you have to write.

- Who would benefit from reading your article? Who would be most interested?

- What kind of readers would select your article from a variety of articles?

Now rank all those potential readers in order, beginning with the readers that would get the most benefit.

## Matching Readers to What They Read.

A close look at magazines in the library or a bookstore will show you where articles listed about or related your topic have already been published. The readers of the articles are the most likely readers of your article.

Make a list of every article on the topic in print for at least the past three years, plus where and when it appeared.

Now look at the masthead, call or write to see if they take freelance submissions. If so, request that a "writer's guidelines" sheet be sent to you. These sheets will tell you about format and size requirements for your topic as well as payment information and billing contacts.

This may seem like allot of effort, but remember you are selling your time, and just sending out blind queries is very inefficient!

## Create a Publications List.

Once you have found the most obvious markets for your topic, and have located it in other publications, you must now dig deeper both to expand on the markets and to find additional sources for searching.

A lot of this work is already done, all you need to do is retrace your steps and modify and expand on the earlier steps. This will now serve as the base for your final market list and "source list" on the subject.

## Study the Publications.

The whole purpose of matching of readers to reading material and searching is to prepare a market list. All the information that you have gathered will now enable you to rank the publishers on the list from most likely and faster response, to the least.

Do you need specific information about the publication in order to fully evaluate it?

The *Over 65: Writing for Pleasure and Profit!* book recommends that you answer the following seven questions as the final approach to evaluating a prospective publication to be included on your market list.

(Most of this information is included on the "writer's guidelines" sheet that you will receive from the masthead inquiry of outlined in the listing in the *Writer's Market*)

## (1) Does the publication pay upon acceptance or publication?

"*Payment on acceptance*" means the editor pays when he says yes to the manuscript. The typical procedure as follows: you query the idea and receive a "*go-ahead*" and then you complete the research and writing and then send your piece off to the editor. Generally you will get a confirmation letter accepting the work, along with a notice that payment shall be forthcoming, usually in 30 days or the next pay schedule.

With this approach your article quite possibly may never be printed before you are paid. Ideally you would like to be paid and have your work published.

On the other hand, "*payment on publication*" means that the payment isn't made until the publication print the article. Which could be a very long time considering how many articles come across the typical editors desk. If the editor uses it, if the publication stays in business, if the editor remembers to pay this, pay that, that's a lot of ifs!

This could mean six to twelve months before you get paid. And guess what? While it sits there it's frozen. You can't send it in elsewhere, no reprints, no rewrites. Being paid on publications is NOT the way you want to proceed.

## (2) How much does the publication pay for articles as long as yours?

Sometimes this information is listed in the writer's guidelines that are sent to you. Sometimes you can find is information in the Writer's Market, or on the publications website, which categorizes work by type, publication and length. This is what might be expected to be paid and this is only a range. It might be a good place to start as it will keep you away from those publications that don't pay very well.

## (3) Does the publication prefer a query or a direct submission?

The answer to this question is fundamental if you truly want to sell a lot of your work. The only justification for sending an original piece unqueried would be the prospects of simultaneous submissions and the megabuck contract if you hit the lottery. But is it worth the gamble of all that time? The *Over 65: Writing for Pleasure and Profit!* book approach doesn't think so. Remember you can always query a publication that prefers direct submissions, but let's face it, they have a lower motivation to buy your work. Caution!

## (4) How often does the publication come out?

Take a look around, most publications are monthlies. This tells you something about the amount of copy that is typically bought by these publications.

## (5) What percentage of the publication is written by freelancers?

There are several approaches to determining the answer to this question:

One, it's outlined in the writer's guidelines on the their website or in the *Writer's Market* of the publications needs. Or two, you can review the masthead and try to estimate the percentage of material in the publication is written by those listed. This is important to identify those publications which use a greater amount of freelance material and are accustomed to outside submissions, given a choice, go where there is more tendency to buy freelance work.

## (6) What manuscript length does the publication prefer?

This quite often is linked to length, so if you are querying an in-depth article it is important to know that some publications never print articles that exceed 800 words!

So if it needs absolutely 2000 words to make any sense, you need to target another publication.

## (7) Does the publications provide additional information and will edit the article submitted by you?

A lot of this information will be related to the topic itself, and will directly affect whether it will become awed as 'hot' property for the publication. This kind of information will come from reading the publications themselves and how they have tailored the content to fit their readership.

A gut sense about how your article will do compared to others is often determined just by going back and spending some time objectively reading the publication.

## What have you got to lose?

## Prepare Your Market List.

Now that you have identified the readers and what the publications are that they read, you can use all of this information to develop a market list that will allow you to query from the 'best" possible sale to the least.

What are the most important criteria for this list?

That the publication pays. Highlighting those that pay upon acceptance and Money! Rank those on your list from highest to the lowest.

Focus your efforts on the top markets.

What's the worst that can happen? They say no? So what!

Remember you are just beginning, your *Over 65: Writing for Pleasure and Profit!* career and you can probably figure on only 33% of your queries being accepted from the start. Maybe worse! But if you follow our approach and you hit on one, you'll be hooked on the writing game forever!

Perhaps a third criterion for your market list is number of issues. The more the times published per year the more work that is bought.

Once you have this list and have gone through this research carefully, step-by-step, you will be turning your time into profits writing!

## WRITING FEASIBILITY

Once you have a market list, you now need to focus on the article itself.

Specifically you now need to answer the question:

*"Is it feasible to write the article you promised in the query?"*

Which would be easy to answer if you promised very little in the query, yet to sell an idea you can't be too vague. It has to get the editors interest, perhaps with quotes, some facts, an anecdote, etc. But no less important, it must be accurate.

If you are a true writer this part should be easy. If you are going to make a living out of being creative and accurate and you should be able to fill up volumes of page with insightful, lively and well-honed words.

---

**Tip:** *Determine what you can provide in the final form and what little tidbits you can add to make the query sell all that much faster.*

---

## Reviewing the Material in Print.

We suggest you do this for two reasons:

(1)  To see how the articles are organized, format and what kinds of sources the other writers cited, and,

(2)  You can then identify sources for comparable quotations, books and/or other references.

The purpose of this effort is to gleem from the publication to determine if there is anything you haven't already thought of as a way to go about your article.

## Compiling a Source List.

Your "source list" contains the three components of all articles:

*Facts, quotes and anecdotes*; The essential ingredients of every article.

You can organize this any way you want, the point is to gather the information in an organized fashion that is at your fingertips as soon as you are given the "*go-ahead*" for a particular piece.

## Analyze your Target Publications.

All that remains now, before writing your query, is it tailor the information at hand about the subject topic from your market list.

To know what material to use and how to present this to the editor.

The best way do this is to read three issues of your target publication, cover to cover.

Ask yourself, who is reading this publication? The advertisements will tell you.

The people that buy those products and services will read your articles.

This sense of the readership and what the publication has been printing in the last three months will give you the "slant" and/or angle that you need for your article.

Very important in both your article and your query are to include some amount of humor.

---

**Tip:** *Remember your query letter is a preview of the material to be covered in your article. It should mention some of your examples, your purpose and the means that you will convey your prospective. All done in the style that you will use in the final piece when it is accepted.*

---

## Final thoughts.

You never realize how much you don't know about a subject or topic until you have to bring an idea you had in your head to life to the query form when you make your proposal to the editor.

You will then discover how much you really know about the topic. You will repeatedly feel ignorant about your subject.

Yet still, despite all of these feelings, you still want to write for money and furthermore, life is too short just write about things you already know about or only those subjects that interest you.

Look at it from both a profit perspective and a learning perceptive combined, you are writing about something you have determined readers wanted to read and the publications want to pay for and you are expending your own personal knowledge about your world at the same time.

# Indeed, two respectable motivations to write!

Below is an article queried and compiled after writing a source list and conducting a market feasibility. Both the author and the readers learned a lot from this process! (OUTSOURCING FACILITY MANAGERS: Design Journal):

### OUTSOURCING FACILITY MANAGERS: (Partial Text)

The question of the use of outside consultants to handle increased or peak workloads and complex projects is now surfacing as an important issue as we approach the year 2013:

Why corporations don't need to carry the overhead.

There are several issues corporations consider when deciding whether to use outside consultants for facility management or build in-house staff to handle corporate facility requirements.

Specifically, when corporations do not have the personnel to allocate the time and resources necessary to manage a project immediately. For example, the requirements might be as simple as monitoring the occupancy levels in various buildings where lease issues are up for consideration. In this case, rather than pull staff off of other assignments, its fairly simple to go to an outside consultant.

Most corporations don't carry specific expertise and sometimes need it immediately. Particularly, design and construction capabilities. This has recently affected such companies such as Sun Microsystems with their rapid growth, Lockheed and their merger with Martin Marrietta, and Hewlett-Packard during their reorganization and downsizing.

When a project a company is facing is filled with in-house subjectivity, decisions that might be arrived at rationally cannot be made. This is frequently the case in major facility relocations or with a corporate headquarters location issue. These can be very emotional issues: Do they stay in the existing area or move to another? It is almost impossible for the in-house facility decision makers to assess the project objectively. The company gets caught up in the emotionalism of the issue and needs some objective outside advice.

In some corporations the facility managers lack information and need to make quick decisions. For example, on a recent project for Xerox Corporation, the company wanted to build a headquarters facility and acquire some additional space on adjacent property. What were the potential facility configurations for the site? A corporation could burn up a lot of staff time having them analyze the possibilities, but more logically an outside consultant could more efficiently provide the solutions.

In-house facility managers have difficulty weighing alternatives and are not always qualified to determine which ones to choose. It is extremely difficult to identify which of several alternatives might be best for the company... etc.

As a consultant, I always ask, "What is in the best interests of the client? As to the value of in-house facility managers, I submit that the question should be: "What is in the best interests of the Company?"

By addressing some of the many issues in process of determining whether outsourcing is a viable solution for corporations, at least some of the wrong decisions can be avoided, and as H. L. Mencken once observed: "there are always easy solutions to every problem; neat, plausible and wrong".

My discussion does not, unfortunately, give any neat and plausible solutions, but rather, sheds some light on the conundrum of in-house facility managers versus outside consultants.

# Chapter 5

## Query and Cover Letters and Responding to Replies

*"Plus ca change, le plus c'est la même chose."*
*"The more things change,*
*the more they stay the same."*
*"Changement est normal."*
*"Change is normal."*
**-French views on life**

## The difference between being an amateur and a professional in the writing world is how you write your query letter.

The biggest chances for success come from knowing what a query letter is - and what it must contain. Once you have got this concept learned the only thing stopping you for achieving your success is energy and desire.

On the face writing skill is what makes the query letter work. If you can't compose a query letter as good as the article that you are proposing then there won't be any writing and checks to follow.

*"Go-ahead"* responses come from query letters that jump, sparkle, persuade, convince, reveal, provoke and ignite an editor's interest in your topic. Query letters sell your idea and you the writer who is going to write about it. You've got to write so clear and appealing that the editor would have to be crazy if he didn't want to see more of your writing.

In other words, don't waste your time or that of the editor that you are sending your query to.

## What are they looking for?

Quick, sharp letters preferably one page, but a maximum of two pages, that tells them:

(1)   What you want to write about,

(2)   How you are going to go about it and what it will contain,

(3)   Maybe whether it will be straight or humorous,

(4)   Why their readers would be interested,

(5)   What your qualifications are, if necessary,

(6)   If you are a person has been in print before and where, and,

(7)   Whether any photos are being provided, if available.

Keep in mind, writing in this letter is almost as important as the content:

- Is it accurate and detailed?

- Is it interesting and to the point?

- And are you writing to the level of their publication?

Writing the query letter that gets you chosen takes hard work, editing and re-editing, plucking and adding until you have pushed every possible editor's button and have written clearly and well.

The query letter is written in business form, no indentations to start paragraphs, and a colon after the salutation.

It is a business letter. You are selling your services to prepare an article about an idea you think the editor's readership will buy. So this letter is business in both content and form. Which means that the letter is written for a purpose, to sell your idea.

## It must meet all of the following criteria to receive a positive response from your query (pardon the redundancy, but this stuff is important):

- What do you want to write about?

- What will the article contain?

- Will the article be straight or humorous?

- Why would the readers be interested in your article?

- What are your qualifications for writing this article?

- Where and when have you been in print before?

- Do you have photographs to sell with the article?

## When you finally finish with your query letter it has to pass the following tests:

- Would a professional write this kind of letter?

- Is your letter concise, complete, to the point and positive? Does it show attention to accuracy and detail?

- Is it convincing the editor that the article should be written?

## NON-fiction books.

Query letters for nonfiction books differ from queries for articles.

Primarily more in terms of scope and depth, than in structure and intent.

When writing a book there is more at stake-the publisher's money and much more of your time, so the query letter is a bigger sales job to do.

And in order to do it, the letter will be twice as long and include several important attachments.

## What kind of attachments?

Perhaps a synopsis but surely a table of contents and a reference/resource page (and others as needed), i.e.:

(1)   An edited list of your publications,

(2)   A resume focusing on your qualifications too prepare the book, and,

(3)   Even a list available photos.

The synopsis of the book's content is often the core of the query letter itself.

And the table of contents shows the framework of the book and outlines the order you are going to proceed with its development. The table of content shows the publisher that rather than a fleeting thought quickly scribbled out on a piece of paper, you have a reasoned, developed idea, like the frame of an exciting new house.

All that is keeping you from completion and sale is the publisher to underwrite its financing.

A reference/resource sheet helps to convince the editor, that your book will grow from solid substance and research. The list will show your familiarity with the general academic text, papers, and authorities in the field and how they relate to what you will prepare.

---

**Tip:** *Finding markets and sending chapters. Specific information about nonfiction book publishers is contained in the book publishers section of the Writer's Market and the respective publishers' website. The question of which book publisher is right for you comes from doing a feasibility study, (discussed in the previous chapter) which must you must do here too, though with obvious modifications.*

---

The difference here is to go to the internet and/or library and write down all of the books that are similar to the one that you are proposing. Keep a tally of the number of books printed by each publisher.

## This list shall be your marketing guide.

Now check it against the top-selling publishers in the field, they are the ones to go after. Query one editor at a time, sending your letter, the attachments and a SASE. (Stamped, self-addressed envelope)

When you receive the "go-ahead", usually you will be asked to submit some representative chapters. And often a contract will follow after the approval of these chapters.

You generally will receive payment at several milestones, as follows: after chapter approval, upon delivery of the final draft and when the book is printed.

Advances. Are payments are basically funds against the royalties which are a percentage of the book's list or price. For your information, royalties are usually 10-15%.

## Some additional things to think about.

• Would it be easier to self-publish?

• Should a resume accompany your query?

Tip: Remember the fastest way to making money is to follow The Over 65: Writing for Pleasure and Profit! book guidelines for writing queries and getting as many as you can out there at one time.

---

**Tip:** *Remember the fastest way to making money is to follow The Over 65: Writing for Pleasure and Profit! book guidelines for writing queries and getting as many as you can out there at one time.*

---

## IMPROVE YOUR QUERY ODDS!

## Cover Letter for "Simultaneous Submissions".

The cover letter plays a less crucial role in selling your writing than the query letter. Primarily because it accompanies the actual manuscript and the editor can read the piece and judge for himself if they want to proceed and enter into a contract.

The purpose of the cover letter is to introduce the copy, display some of its contents, discuss possible illustrations, perhaps talk about the rights offered, and suggest others ideas you might include as sidebars to enhance the topic, and also indicate whether you want the manuscript back.

## "Simultaneous submission" cover letters are sent for following selling scenarios:

Multiple submissions to editors of newspaper travel sections,

Newspaper weekly supplements,

Religious magazines,

Regional publications,

In-flight magazines,
And to sell reprints.

## There are two approaches to writing the cover letter:

The *short cover letter* which physically covers the top half of the front page of the copy. Which are purely the bare essentials while drawing the editors' attention to the text itself, to be drawn in by the words and images and immediately send it off to be printed.

This approach has five functions: (all to be done in about 5" of space)

(1)   Tell them who you are with your name and address

(2)   What is the copy about, summarizing the contents

(3)   How you can be reached by phone or fax or email address

(4)   Do you have any photos or illustrations that might accompany the text to follow

(5)   And if you want the manuscript returned

Second approach: The *full page cover letter* is done when you have a message you want to convey that simply can't be done with a short note or, if you are submitting just to magazine editors whose pace is a bit less hectic.

The first two paragraphs sell the copy and the rest looks like the shorter note but longer.

## What's the advantage?

More space let's you go into more detail about the merits of the piece and the accompanying photos or illustrations. You can also use a full letterhead of your stationary if you wish.

Again the whole idea is to sell the article or copy that accompanies the letter. The size is directly related to publication and the amount of information that you think you need to get the job of selling your piece done.

The writing in the cover letter must be concise, and as enticing as the article that is attached.

Below is a query letter from the nonfiction book submission reference to earlier (Charles Baudelaire: Life in Paris):

### The Query Follow-up Proposal Letter:

January 2, 2012

To: Book Publishing Press
    Santa Fe Avenue
    Main Street, California 94123

Attn: Mrs. You Know Who, Publisher

Dear You Know:

Hope this finds you well and looking forward to a great year!

As we have discussed, here is my revised proposal for the book about ABC.

This revised approach is now focused specifically on both the chronological and geographical importance of his life and work in Industry.

I believe it is now more centered in response to your earlier comments and consistent with the 'Business Place Series' concept. Of course, it will need additional 'tweaking' as I move forward with assembling exhibits, graphics and content.

Below, you will find the following revised items:

1.  Proposed Table of Contents

2.  Draft content for a few illustrative Sites and the Introduction, with selected works included for context.

3.  Examples pictures of Sites and Details.

4.  A Timeline which serves as a yardstick for the development and direction of the book.

As I mentioned before, we should be able to get a cover Endorsement or Foreword Introduction from literary expert; Dr. I Know You, who has written a book about this subject work among others.

Looking forward to hearing from you soon.

Thanks in advance for your consideration.

Regards,


Author ABC

# *Chapter 6*

## Structure

*"Begin at The beginning and go on till you come to The end; Then stop."*
**-Lewis Carroll**

When your query gets a "*go-ahead*", you have typically about three weeks to get the finished copy to the editor. Sometimes the editor will give you some other deadline in which case that would revise this schedule.

Nothing sacred about the three weeks, but most editors feel that if the copy doesn't arrive in this time frame, then, it may never arrive.

So, from the standpoint of being responsible about your *Over 60: Writing for Pleasure and Profit!* writing career you might as well stick to this deadline. It should be plenty of time because you have already done your research and a lot of your footwork during the feasibility study.

What now remains is the final research, the writing and the mailing.

## Most importantly putting STRUCTURE to your piece.

## Researching.

A few more days of research will fill in any holes you might have left in your Feasibility study.

To determine what you need at this point is go directly to copies of the publication that you are going to be writing for so you can produce an article utilizing the same or similar selling characteristics.

Imitate it in terms of its quality, and to some degree, form, and then the chances are excellent that your article will be bought.

## You're looking for structure.

- Why are the articles set up the way they are?
  (Specifically sentence length, type of lead paragraph and length and how the piece is concluded).

- Is the piece written in the first person or the third?

- Who is quoted? And how many quotes are in each article?

- Are the articles funny or are the straightforward and informational?

- What question does the article answer?

- Is it asked in the lead?

Determine the working question that was the premise for the article and from that, will come the secondary questions which will give the piece internal organization.

## Now go about setting up your outline.

Start with your *"working question"* and ask yourself some of the *"secondary question"*.

Try to develop some order: chronological, region, etc. whatever makes sense and is already the format of the publication.

Then step back and ask the following about each question:

Do the readers care? Is it important?

Answers to these questions will determine whether these questions are relevant, or even retained as part of the piece.

- How are you going to go about answering these questions?

- Through fact, quote or anecdote?

- Again, what is the typical format of the other articles in the publication?

- Where will you find these three elements?

- Take a look at your source list. Have you gathered enough information and material?

- Is this the best you can find?

- Is it up to date?

- Is it to the point and interesting?

**Remember:** You have received the "go-ahead" which is just a way of saying: "Ok, let me see it". Now you must produce the best copy possible.

Now you are ready to write.

## Writing.

This explanation is going to take some time, so please bear with us.

The *Over 65: Writing for Pleasure and Profit!* book believes this section will still be shamefully short, because in effect, this chapter is not really teaching you how to write as it is teaching to sell what you write.

And as you sell more and more, your writing will keep getting better and better as the motivation of being paid for your efforts and seeing your name in print will inspire to continue to sharpen your writing skills.

### You need to read at least ten articles about the subject you are going to write about for the publication.

This analytical approach will help you figure out how to organize your idea and express it in words that the readers will find appealing.

How could any book tell you how to write for all the thousands of publications needing your words?

Just let the writers in the publications that you are writing for show what has been bought, then repeat the approach they used and you will take their place in the coming issues.

Basically, this part of the book is a "*do-it-yourself*" learning procedure.

What you learn and how, is entirely up to you.

## Structure.

## First of all, nothing is more important than the "*lead*" of the article.

The first paragraph is what the sells the piece to the editor and to the readers.

Another word for it is the "*hook*". It grabs the reader.

Keep your leads to one sentence or two. This sets the tone for the article, and creates the mood and/or the spirit for what is going to follow.

Study what has been used in other issues of the magazine and stick close to their lead and use it as a guideline.

Sometimes you don't have to write the lead first, just start writing and the lead will come to you later.

On the other hand, write 10 to 15 leads, even before a rough body of the text is completed. Then go back and select the one that best suits the rest of the piece.

## Make a few revisions; spice it up a bit, and, Viola! There you go!

The next element is the "*transitional paragraph*", this is the paragraph that gets you from the lead and into the text of the piece and is generally the road map of how the piece is going to evolve and how it will get there.

These next few paragraphs are often the vehicles that straighten out a distorted lead and establish the true tone of the piece.

This transitional paragraph often tells how the discussion in the piece will be presented, i.e. chronologically, region, steps of development, etc.

It is sometimes referred to as the "*bridge*", since it links the lead to the body of the work through the use of conjunctive thoughts.

Without a well-designed bridge perhaps most articles would make little sense.

You need to study your 10 articles from the publication you are writing for closely. How are they structured with the lead and the bridge? It can be the difference between selling your piece and a lot of your words going nowhere!

Make the "*body*" of your piece paragraphs proportional to the size of your lead and the transitional paragraph.

When in doubt don't go beyond 2 to 3 sentences in length.

(Books, on the other hand, have longer paragraphs than articles.)

The "*conclusion*" is also very important.

There is no trick to writing conclusions. You can't just leave your reader hanging and you need to resolve the fundamental question and secondary questions.

---

**Tip:** *If you are having trouble coming up with an ending, just repeat a word or phrase from the lead that can comfortably be repeated in the final paragraph. You've seen this a hundred times in publications you have been reading for years you just never paid any attention to it. Repeating a phrase or word that was stated in the beginning gives the reader the feeling that the piece has gone full circle and the journey has ended. You don't have to force it.*

---

This is not a recommendation to use something from the title, but just a reference to it will be satisfactory. The title most often will be changed for newspaper articles (by the editor) to fit space demands and headline form.

In some markets think of the title as the first lead, the title is what pulls the reader into the body of the article. Once there, the reader will stay with the article as long as the content stays with the title, sustains interest and doesn't have any large amount of copy block that obstructs comprehension. (Maybe like this chapter?… sorry about that, you have to keep up!)

A good title tells what the article or piece is about. If it is humor, there is a feeling of the level of humor in the piece itself. The best humor titles come from the heart of the material. Editors rarely change humor titles.

## Now for the finished article.

Ask your friends or someone in your family about the title only. Ask them from the title what they think the piece is about.

The structure basics outlined here are the most important elements of writing a piece of copy that sells.

Don't worry, no two articles are ever done the same, or, are bought from the same publications.

# Chapter 7

## Plot and Purpose

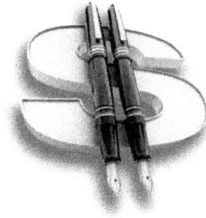

*"Do not arouse The wrath
of The great and powerful Oz!…
Pay no attention to The man
behind The curtain."*
**-from "Wizard of Oz"**

## Every story or article starts with a question that is answered in the climax or conclusion.

Writing comes easy to you. The right words just seem to flow off your fingertips, lifting you to incredible heights of creative pleasure.

In one quiet morning you can invoke the autumn setting of whirling dry leaves and bright clouds piled high into the sky, and in that setting you come up with the most enchanting characters - *a bearded, graying old man sitting on a park bench clasping an acorn in his worn leather glove hand.*

You have a knack for taking these rich descriptions and weaving them with dialogue between the old man and his dog about dreams unfulfilled that can make a reader sob all over the pages.

## And what about plot and structure?

Best way to address this issue is to look at screenplays.

Screenwriters understand plot and structure better than any other type of writer.

---

**Tip:** *Screenwriters are always answering the Major Dramatic Question. (Or the "MDQ"). It's the simple truth about sitcoms and a tightly structured novel. Shakespeare knew it and the storytellers who used to sit around the crackling fire knew it.*

---

## Simple. Absolutely Simple.

It bears repeating; every story or article basically begins with a question and in the conclusion, answers it.

When you start to write your story or article, the idea needs to have a setting, characters, time frame (period), style and theme.

But you should always be thinking of the critical MDQ, the skeleton to hang everything else on.

**Let's state this clearly, if you haven't begun to think about the MDQ, you really haven't begun any substantial writing on your piece.**

Let's back up a little.

• Think again about the old man in the park. The old man and the acorn.

• What's going on in his head?

• Did he have a family?

• Where's his wife?

• Why is he reminiscing about his lost potential?

• Is there a connection to the unrealized potential in the acorn in his hand?

Viola! There it is! The MDQ!

• Will this man realize how absolutely powerful he once was –like the acorn?

• What will he do if he comes to that realization and knows he can still change his life?

There you go. Now you've got the skeleton of a story.

But the concept of a story or an article is more than just the bones, there has to be the rest of the body, the rest of the plot and structure.

## Possible other elements are as follows:

- Tension

- Conflict

- Paradox

- Complications

- Obstacles

There are lots of ways to look at each of these elements, however, the *Over 65: Writing for Pleasure and Profit!* book approach has devised a method to address each that should serve as a descriptive guideline to help develop your idea or topic to the next level.

*Tension* is the condition that already exists when your article or story starts off.

Tension is what makes us grind our teeth in our sleep; it's the tensions in the story that holds our attention.

Getting back to our story again:

*Perhaps the old man sighs because he thinks of his past glory and mistakes and wonders what will become of him.*

*We then learn that he has just had a daughter who was diagnosed with cancer and he worries about her health and if he will be able to help.*

There lies the tension.

Often you need to look for conflict. The conflict is the result of the interaction between the present circumstances and the strong need of the main character or main story line.

What's the *conflict* in our story?

*Maybe the old man had a wife who died of cancer and he always regretted not being there when she needed him because he had left her and gone off for his own selfish reasons earlier their marriage.*

*Now he doesn't want the same thing to happen with his daughter, yet he doesn't have the resources to get to where she lives in another city.*

Now we need to add the paradox.

*Ambivalence* can stir up tremendous incidents of paradox. A degree of ambivalence is present in every person.

*Perhaps our old man character is torn. Knowing that he wasn't there for most of his daughters' life and wondering what good it will do anyway to go and see her.*

*Besides he is not a doctor and cancer is an evil illness. Yet, on the other hand, he needs to satisfy the inner feelings of regret for walking out of his daughter's life and not being there when his wife passed away.*

Consider now the *complications* and *obstacles*.

These are the elements that come into your story or article and heighten the interest.

They are the roadblocks that keep getting in the way own the main story line or the main character.

Preventing the story from going as planned or keeping the main character from getting what he ultimately wants. Complications should always be organized in order of increasing intensity. By introducing each obstacle will make reaching his goal or the climax/conclusion, that much more fulfilling.

When writing a story or article begin by making a list of the possible things that could go wrong for your main character, in our case the old man, from minor inconveniences to major tragedies.

Our list might look something like this:

- Missing the bus

- Money worries, saving to take a job

- Having to deal with an abusive boss

- Living in a slum hotel

- Heavy rain and worn shoes

- Mugged while counting his last savings

- Hearing that his daughter illness is getting worse

- Running out of time

---

**Tip:** *Some writers worry about over planning a story or article but we want you to sell what you write, yet we don't want you to be fearing that outlining a plot and structure will ruin your story's spontaneity. The best you can expect to do is when you finish writing your auricle or story that you have answered the fundamental question and then resolve the other issues that are brought up in the storyline.*

---

## It's simple, have you answered the MDQ?

Keep in mind this plot process will take a while to work through.

Not at just one sitting, sometimes gallons of coffee (if your doctor or cardiologist says its ok after your last triple bi-pass), sometimes it can take days.

## Remember, writing is 90% thinking and 10% scribbling.

It's not enough for you to just create images and move your readers to tears or action.

Plot and story Structure go much deeper, to somewhere deep inside of us, and once we have mastered it, we can create worlds in which our characters and dialogue become unforgettable.

Below is the screenplay "Pendulum" highlighting the use of plot and structure:

### Pendulum: A Screenplay

Stare deeply into the watery blue eyes of an elderly and wheelchair bound man, pull back and you'll find yourself surrounded by the serenity of the manicured lawn of the Thousand Oaks Convalescent Hospital… his home for the past 30 years.

Physical examinations must be done periodically, as with all of the elderly. For David Johnson, it's an opportunity to briefly escape the confines of this limited world. Today's ambulance ride with his nurse and confidant, Angela Ryan, to Lakeview General Hospital will be unlike any other… it will alter his life forever… embarking on mankind's most impossible dream… a second chance… to go through life again knowing what he knows now.

On the way to the hospital there is a terrible accident, a collision between the ambulance and a careening eighteen wheeler out of control! Angela is thrown clear, and David… a concussion and deep lacerations; he is fortunate. Tests are done, and their conclusions are shocking. It seems as though David's cells are multiplying at an alarming rate, reversing metabolically to such an extent that he is actually regressing in age!

He may only have six months to live, as the physiological trauma of the regeneration process is determined to be too much for his life support systems.

Further tests are performed: His condition constantly monitored by his faithful nurse. His injuries heal at an astonishing rate! While visually he begins to appear noticeably younger, he goes through spells of strength and coherence then lapses into unexplainable periods of severe pain and near death states. Angela reviews his records, and finds nothing regarding his past! No family contacts, no prior addresses, no medical information prior to his admittance on October 11, 1958. She suspects foul play and has him transferred out of Thousand Oaks.

With the assistance of a retired ex-cop turned private investigator, Vince Carpeski, and a curious friend, Dr. Conrad Hoffman, an unresolved mysterious and suspenseful trail of a medical cover-up is revealed! The case was thought to have been sealed thirty years ago with the murder of a prominent hospital chief-of-staff surgeon who was on the verge of going public with damaging research fraud allegations. A multi-million dollar pharmaceutical firm, Medtech, is implicated. A desperate man of corruption and greed, Syd Underwood, is found to have masterminded the scheme.

As David and Angela race against time in their search for answers and truth, a once-in-a-lifetime love is rediscovered; a "fountain of youth" becomes a reality, giving love a chance to blossom again. If only for amount, medical technology reaches into the future, sending shivering moments of enlightenment to strike deep onto the soul, as justice is served! The story swings between the forces of good and evil, eternal hope and despair as the PENDULUM swings to an engaging and masterfully written climax, offering our hearts and dreams... the possibility... of a second chance.

EXT. TWO LANE ROAD... DAY

The ambulance cruising along on a not-so-busy road... lights not flashing.

INT. AMBULANCE

Jon in his wheelchair, Angela sitting beside him.

                    JON

I don't need an ambulance.

                    ANGELA

It's more convenient... and it's paid for.

JON

Can they at least flip on the lights?

ANGELA

(not amused)

That's illegal.

CUT TO:

EXT. THREE-WAY INTERSECTION… UTILITY POLE

A WORKMAN atop a utility pole, malting adjustments to a transformer. On one of the streets, up a hill, a gas tanker. On the other, in the distance, the ambulance coming into view.

INT. CAB… 18-WHEELER

A TRUCKER behind the wheel, 30s, unshaven and proudly sporting a beer belly. The Rolling Stones blares over the speakers as he directs with his cigarette while attempting to drive.

EXT. 18 WHEELER

As the truck passes, two bumpers tickers: "Smokers Are People Too!" and "My Child Beat Up Your Honor Student."

INT. AMBULANCE

JON

(sarcastic)

If I'm good, will I get a lolly?

ANGELA

Lighten up a little, will you? Going to the doctor should be fun…a way of getting outside.

JON

Easy for you to Say.

INT. CAB ... 18-WHEELER

The trucker SEES the intersection at the bottom of the hill...the workman and a RED LIGHT. He PRESSES his foot on the Brake, but the tanker DOES NOT RESPOND! FRANTICALLY PUSHING THE BRAKES, NOTHING HAPPENS!

EXT. THREE-WAY INTERSECTION

Watching the inevitable... the 18-wheeler swaying back and forth as the driver tries to slow its momentum.

INT. AMBULANCE

ANGELA

It'd make it a lot better if you...

Angela's thought INTERRUPTED by the 18-wheeler SLAMMING into the Ambulance. The back door FLIES open and Angela is THROWN onto the lawn of a nearby house. The ambulance veers out of control before CRASHING into the utility pole... throwing the WORKMAN onto the lawn. The pole CREAKS as it prepares to fall a LIVE WIRE swings menacingly back and forth over the ambulance.

The 18-WHEELER continues on and HITS a fire hydrant, causing it to spray the ambulance with water. The tanker then SMASHES into a parked car and ROLLS onto its side... sending the cigarette into the street. Gasoline GUSHES out of the tanker and it ROLLS towards the cigarette.

The AMBULANCE DRIVER, meanwhile, doesn't appear to be conscious... his bloody arm dangles through the broken front window and limply asks for help. The WORKMAN scrambles to his truck and removes a cellular phone. He then runs away from the accident and begins dialing.

The cigarette, meanwhile, quietly rests in the street. The injured TRUCKER looks up to see the cigarette and gasoline MAKE CONTACT.

The resulting FIRE quickly spreads over to the tanker and BOOM… the tanker and driver erupt into a ball of fire.

The explosion ROCKS the ground, the utility pole FALLS, and the live wire MAKES CONTACT with the ambulance RESULTING in a huge ELECTRICAL SHOCK. The ambulance VIBRANTLY GLOWS with electricity.

The Utility Worker frantically YELLS into the cellular telephone. After being electrified for five or ten seconds, the Ambulance STOPS glowing power is out in the whole neighborhood. The Utility Worker stops shouting and stares in astonishment at the scene of destruction.

FADE TO:

INT. LAKEVIEW GENERAL DAY

Jon in the intensive care unit at Lakeview General, a maze of tubes enshrouds his body…a bandaged head, his left arm in a cast, and breathing through a respirator. Angela enters the room, scrapes and bruises adorn parts of her body and she also wears a cast over her left wrist. But at least she's walking. Jon speaks slowly… it is painful for him to talk.

                              ANGELA

You're really quite lucky.

                               JON

I don't feel lucky. Looks like you drew the Royal Flush,

                              ANGELA

My wrist doesn't think so, at least you didn't end up like Martin… or the man in the truck.

                               JON

Who's Martin?

ANGELA

The ambulance driver,

JON

Is he...

Jon doesn't need to finish the sentence...he knows the result.

ANGELA

He had a wife and two kids.

JON

How old was he?

ANGELA

Twenty-eight. The kids are two and four. Two girls.

JON

How's the...

He doesn't want to ask.

ANGELA

You should just be glad your injuries aren't worse.

JON

I'm surprised it doesn't hurt more.

# *Chapter 8*

## The Rewrite Process

*"Past performance is no indication of future results."*

**-Unknown source**

Of all the friends and writers that have used this method over the years, the *Over 65: Writing for Pleasure and Profit!* book has found the one and only thing they all had in common was that they all needed to do more work. Always.

## Good writing is the result of rewriting.

No writer ever gets a piece of writing completely right the first time.

Writers must keep refining and rewriting and rethinking their work until the piece is as good as they can make it.

An editor that you have sent it into may read it and say:

*"It's not the proper time to run this piece but the writing is excellent!"*

You must be very honest with yourself about the way you write.

Don't ever kid yourself that there isn't any word that can't be changed to make it better, yet, at the same time, try not to agonize over your choice of words in the meantime as you write.

Because you'll never experience the satisfaction of the pleasure during the rewrite process. (Did I say pleasure?)

## True writers feel the final revision is the joy.

Once you've got something - or anything down on paper. You can almost immediately see what's wrong with it. You'll find it best to go through what you've written several times.

Looking at the pace, setting, facts, etc. Otherwise, you get so caught up in the article or story and end up patting yourself on the back instead of really looking at what you've written and slashing and rewriting.

## The Rewrite Approach.

## First, you need to just scan over your piece rather than read.

Check what's happening on each page, in each paragraph, to make sure the beginning is not to slow, too choked with words and concepts.

Try to see where the piece actually starts and where it moves to the middle and whether the beginning makes any sense.

- Does the article or story get underway with the first sentence?

- Is the setting clear?

- Is it obvious which way the piece is headed?

- And are the characters visible and interesting?

- Look at the middle, ask yourself is anything happening? If not, then you need to go over this part very carefully.

- Are you following the laws of cause and effect?

- Tension and conflict?

- Is the piece motivated to answer the fundamental question?

- Is the pace OK?

- Will the reader want to continue to turn to the next page?

- If it's a story, does each chapter end with an exciting point or suspense, so that the reader will be eager to turn to the next page?

## Now, take a look at the ending.

- Does it seem satisfying, believable, convincing and motivated?

- Does the piece drag on or does the piece end too quickly?

- Are all of the secondary questions answered?

- Does it give your readers time to savor the ending?

- If it was going to be so easy to solve all the issues than why did it take so long to end?

## Transitions are almost always tested during the rewrite process.

Sometimes you need to decide if you should just leave a gap or extra space to indicate the time gap, and then start on with the next thought or scene.

Check for the continuity of details in your writing, are the descriptions of the characters, place, clothing, etc. the same in each paragraph or scene?

## Then you've finished with all this troubleshooting, and dealt with-the major issues in the rewriting.

Now you need to go through the piece word-by-word, rereading from beginning to end with a critical eye, tinkering as you go.

## What is your purpose?

- Now you are making sure of what you said and you are checking your facts:

- Did you spell all the names and places correctly?

- How does the writing sound?

- Are the rhythms feeling good?

- Are there too many sentences in the same form?

- How about the characters, do they all seem the same?

- Are they alive?

- Can you actually visualize them?

- What about the dialogue? Read it aloud does it sound right?

Here is where you need to rely on your inner ear. Edit the dialogue wherever possible; take out unnecessary comments or anything that might seem trivial or boring.

## Viewpoint.

Is it clear whose viewpoint you're in? Or do you jump around from first person to third and beyond. (Some point of views are better left alone.)

Now it should go without saying, but you should be looking for grammatical and/or spelling errors.

---

**Tip:** *And of course, there is punctuation, but some editors have different terms and styles, so you need to review carefully the writer's guidelines you obtained during the research and feasibility study. Always give the editors requirements the benefit of the doubt.*

---

Also check for word repetitions, and take out redundant words: and, "*well, just and very*".

Finally, after doing all the necessary revisions, now you need to read the whole article or story through again without stopping.

If it still holds your interest, then you can bet it will hold the editors and the readers as well.

Before you send your article or story off to the editor it should be the best possible writing you can do.

## It is your "writer's responsibility"...

## Summary Checklist for Rewriting:

## Beginning.

- Is the beginning too slow?

- Is it clear and concise?

- Anything happening?

- Does it move?

- And above all else, is it interesting?

## Middle.

- Have you followed the rules of:

- Cause and effect,

- Tension and conflict?

- Again, is anything happening?

- Are there breaks and transitions?

- Is it interesting to read?

## Conclusion/endings.

- Is the ending too slow? Too rapid?

- Have you written somewhere beyond the actual ending?

- Is the ending interesting?

- Does it answer the MDQ?

- The fundamental questions?

## General.

- Have you been efficient with words?

- Have you used too many adjectives and adverbs?

- Have you used strong nouns and active verbs?

- Is there anything cliché that you can omit?

- Is the chronology correct?

- Are all the transitions smooth and believable?

- Is the viewpoint clear and consistent?

- Will your reader turn every page?

- Is something important happening or being said?

- Have you checked all the facts for accuracy?

- Have you edited the dialogue enough?

- Have you left any questions unanswered?

- Is the spelling and grammar correct?

- Are you pleased with the result?

Below is an example of a nonfiction "rewrite" process:

### The Zodiac Project: Prologue

As you begin to read this book, I'd like you to keep an open mind, as this is not a traditional book. I'd like you to ask yourself to evaluate your life. More specifically, I'd like you to ask yourself if you are happy?

Of course, your definition of happiness will depend upon who you are — but do you have a sense of peace in your heart, a feeling of security about your future, and a feeling of anticipation when you wake up in the morning? If we can call this happiness, then would you say at this moment you are happy?

I think I can safely say that not that many people will be able to reply with a resounding yes. Most people are unable to say their life is everything they had hoped it would be. What is it that causes us so much unhappiness? What is it that is going on in the world that prevents so many people from simply being happy?

Well, it seems to me that we are living in an age of chaos. Chaos defined as a condition of confusion, indicative of unorganized matter (energy) that existed before the creation of the cosmos.

Simply by going about our lives, we find ourselves worn out and fatigued. Media, newspapers and television bombard us with information, and at work, we face problems and misunderstandings. The sources of our problems seem numerous and overwhelming.

This is likely to be the fact no matter where in the world we are likely to go. This tiny planet of ours is covered with economic conflict, domestic discord, religious wars, ethnic prejudice, environmental distress, and every other type of problem imaginable. And all the bad news about people suffering, people enjoying suffering, people getting richer, people getting poorer, the oppressed and the oppressors, reaches us in a matter of seconds from the opposite side of the globe.

Who? Might we ask, is responsible for all this suffering? The world is becoming an ever more divided, estranged, and complicated place to live. We are already up to our necks in chaos, but the world's troubles seem to be getting deeper and deeper.

One thing we all have in common is that we are all looking for a solution. Everyone is looking for an answer — and it is an answer that is so simple and effective that it has heretofore eluded us.

So what is the cause of all this chaos? What is the center of it all? Perhaps this is an inevitable phenomenon. Though we all belong to the same species, if we live in different places and in different cultures, the way we think is bound to be different.

And to make matters worse, most people have difficulty accepting things that are unlike the things around them. The result is a never ending process of troubles and suffering. It would seem as long as people are people, any solution proposed is certain to come up short.

And so now we are back where we started. Can there ever be a single solution that can apply to all people on the globe, that everyone can be convinced of, and that is so simple that everyone can understand it?

An answer: "Energy"

In fact, I would like to propose an answer, and it is just this: We are nothing more than an assemblage of different types of energies, or molecules. We exist, from the moment we are conceived in our mothers' womb until we pass onto to another life, as energy.

From a physical perspective, humans are energy. When I first realized this I started to look at the world in a whole new way. I realized that this connection to energy applies to all people, and, what I am about to propose in this book can be applied to everyone, all over the world. I believe it is also a way to start to see the way that people should live their lives.

So how can people live happy and healthy lives?

Energy that is moving is like water in a river, it remains pure because it is moving, when energy becomes trapped, like water, it ceases to flourish. Therefore, energy must be constantly moving. When this energy stops moving, the body starts to decay and if the energy stops in your brain, it can be life threatening.

But why does are energy become stagnant? We can think of it as a condition of stagnation of our emotions. Modern researchers have shown that the condition of the mind has a direct impact on the condition of the body. When you are living a full and enjoyable life, you feel better physically, and when your life is filled with struggles and sorrow, your body knows it — you can feel it.

Moving, changing, flowing —

this is what life is about — energy

# Chapter 9

## Preparing Your Work to Send

*"Business has a noble purpose. Making money is one of the important things that business does for society."*
**-John Mackey, CEO of Whole Foods**

## Mailing the copy! Finally the day has arrived to send off your work!

You want your work to arrive as quickly as possible, flat, intact, and undamaged. And you also want to make sure you receive a response with the same positive haste.

## Sending and Mailing.

In order for that to occur you must include a SASE (stamped, self-addressed envelope) large enough to contain the copy plus a reply letter or note. Most editors however, will return your material even if you don't send a SASE, but not doing so will make you sound like an amateur.

SASEs should be the same size as the original envelope, folded in half with postage already affixed. If you don't want the manuscript returned you should at least provide a business sized envelope to return the reply.

If you are sending items abroad you might also include an international reply coupon with a self-addressed envelope so that the editor doesn't have to pay for the reply.

All magazine and newspaper articles and manuscript should be paperclipped (not stapled) and send book manuscripts unclipped.

You should never use those tacky school report covers or binders. Cover letters must be sent with "simultaneous submissions" and they may be necessary for "single submissions" that have not been preceded by a query. These also might also include some filler information and humor, and only if you really have something to add or say about your special expertise on the subject.

Don't just tell the editor that you want them to buy it, they already know that.

Unless there is something special about the contents, rarely do you need a cover letter for queried articles and books.

The outside wrapping should be sturdy enough to protect your work during the rough handling it will surely get on its journey through transit. It should be tightly sealed and include both your return address and the name of the person, with address, where it is being sent.

If you don't know the proper name, you can send it to the appropriate subject editor.

A book manuscript sent abound in a box should include a return address tag and sufficient postage for its return. This should be paper-clipped to the top of the box. Publishers of book rarely use the same wrapping and the same box.

There are cheaper ways to ship and mail, but Priority and First Class are always the best. This way the item arrives in a few days and will be returned quickly in the unlikely event that the publisher folded while you were gathering facts and doing your research.

Don't forget to write "Priority Mail" or "First Class" in large letters on the wrapping so that it is sure to get forwarded that way.

Make sure you keep a copy of everything that you mail, and if for some reason something goes wrong with the delivery, you can always send another copy.

Keep in mind that going to the trouble and expense of sending things Certified and or Registered isn't worth the expense and most editors aren't even impressed by the gesture.

They might even think the worse of you for doing it this way because it might signal that you the writer are afraid that unless the editor signs for it, he might be stealing it and not going to pay.

No editor wants to get involved in any litigation.

If you are mailing photos, make sure you pack large prints inside with cardboard inserts and write in large letters on the envelope: PHOTOS DO NOT BEND. Put a rubber band around the inserts and include your copy in the same envelope. Also send this First Class or Priority Mail. Every photo print or slide that you send should be identified.

And make sure you print or stamp your name on the back of each. Each photo/slide should have a caption/description that numerically corresponds to a photo/slide listing that also has your name and address on it.

Remember: Photos and slides are only sent when they are requested by the editor.

They should not accompany query letters or simultaneous submissions, but are offered during this stage of the process. Do not send any valuable photos or slides unless you have copies.

## Now you need a system for keeping track of your mailings.

The *Over 65: Writing for Pleasure and Profit!* book recommends the following approach:

- Keep your mailing record on a separate sheet of paper, 8 1/2 x 11 with the year and the most recent page number at the top of the page, now allow about an inch and a half below each five or six entries to allow for notations later.

- Record every item, query, or submission when you have mailed it, and likewise, all incoming mail about those items in the entry.

---

**Tip:** *Not only will the mailing record prevent you from sending the same query or copy to the same editor more than once, it will also serve as proof of the volume of work in the event of an IRS audit.*

---

It will also remind you of which editors have not replied, which of those are prompt and buy often, and ultimately how much income you are earning from all your writing.

Finally, a few words in defense of mailing in general. If you don't, you will never sell.

What's the worst that an editor can say? No big deal. The next time those "No's" could turn into a "Yes".

## So get your words in the mail! (or email)

When sending submittals via emails, it is best to use the following approach:

- Make sure you have spelled the email address correctly and always cc yourself so that when your email arrives back to you, you know it was actually send (if the attachments are large, due to some program file size limitations… for example, AOL has this problem, if so, just open a Gmail account and circumvent this issue).

- Include a brief description and date in the message bar, with your name and article/book title.

The cover email references the attachments that are included with the submittal; typically, cover letter/query, Outline, table of contents, synopsis or pitch, first couple of chapters, author bio, etc.

Another good idea is to set your email settings to send you a confirmation that the email you send to the editor has been actually received and opened.

Some email programs don't have this functionality, so politely ask for confirmation in your email from the editor that it has been received.

Nothing cute, just professional and business-like and no annoying smiley faces.

## Now You Wait…

After they are sent, and while they are out there, do something to reward yourself that you did the best job you could.

Remind yourself that you had enough courage to take on the writing world.

# *Chapter 10*

## Writing Legalize: Copyrights, Taxes, Agents, Editors and Other Issues

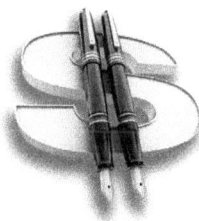

*"I'm not so much concerned about a return upon my money, as I am about a return of my money."*
**-Mark Twain quote**
**(popularized by Will Rogers)**

## Let's face it; it's difficult to be a writer.

First you have to do all this marketing stuff, and then on top of it nothing could be more confusing than your rights and other legal requirements that you must adhere to.

But actually there is little reason to get concerned, anxious or bewildered.

There are two kinds of rights involved with freelance sales.

## *Copyright* is one.

## And *All Rights, First Rights* and *Second Rights* are the other.

They sound similar, but they are significantly different in their purpose and their application.

The *Over 65: Writing for Pleasure and Profit!* book would first like to offer this disclaimer:

*We are not lawyers and if you have a specific question about any of the rights discussed in this Chapter or in the whole book for that matter, you should seek legal counsel.*

## *Copyright* is the most critical issue.

Although it is very straightforward and very easy to register, in the same context, never has a term been more misused than when it is applied to writing.

The typical question we get from most of our readers:

*"Should I copyright my article, script or book?"*

When in fact, the question should be, whether you should register the copyright. You would rarely do this for articles.

The reasoning is this. We are in a common law country (assuming USA where this book is printed), and the rights to the copy come from its creation.

You are obtaining a legal right of ownership from the moment you put the words down on paper.

Should somebody else take your property, sell it or otherwise cause you some sort of financial damage, you could in fact take them to court.

If you could prove that you had actually created the piece, you might have some legal grounds to stand on. In reality, there are probably a hundred ways that the whole matter of proving right of ownership would get convoluted and complicated.

Nevertheless, it's as simple as that.

However, if you had registered the piece by sending the proper forms to Washington, D.C. and placed your copyright symbol on it, your pursuit of legal restitution would be that much easier.

The big difference in court is the other person must prove that he created the piece. Without the copyright you would have to prove you first created something that he copied. Most lawyers will tell that in a court of law that puts you in a much more favorable position.

To register your work costs money and takes time. And also can be counterproductive.

In a strictly business sense, it is worth registering a copyright only when there is possible issue of an legal infringement suit that might be needed to protect earnings.

Most items that you would write would not earn enough to justify going to court in the first place.

---

**Tip:** *The only potentially monetarily lucrative creative pieces usually are the ones to get registered, such as: Music, Scripts books, Software and Newsletters.*

---

Generally magazine editors don't expect you to copyright articles. And no editor worth his salt in words would put your words in print and not pay you for it. He just wouldn't be that stupid.

For literary items the copyright symbol © is followed by its date of creation and the writers name. This symbol tells others that you have exclusive right to do the following:

- To reproduce the copyrighted work into copies.

- To prepare derivative works based on the copyrighted work.

- To distribute the copyrighted work for public sale or by transfer of ownership.

- To display the copyrighted work publicly.

- To perform the copyrighted work publicly.

You can register literary works, but you can't register ideas, procedures, methods, titles, names or short phrases related to the topic you are writing about.

The process for registering your copyright is very straightforward.

You complete the proper copyright form and send the fee and required number of copies of the item to be registered. You then have up to a year to complete the required registration once the item alias been sold or distributed. Similar items written about the same topic in some cases can be included on the same form for the same fee.

## Contract Rights.

More important to you as writer are the contract rights that are purchased with your manuscript or copy.

These become your contractual rights.

They will define how the editor will use your copy and are what is typically defined as the three part definition of a contract:

• *Offer*

• *Consideration*

• *Acceptance*

The contractual rights make all the effort of the general legal copyrighting process specific.

You write a query letter, you make an offer.

What follows is the acceptance.

This is when the editor agrees to buy the article or work.

Somewhere between the offer and the acceptance you should be aware of the rights to that purchase.

Most of these "rights" fall into three categories:

- All rights

- First Rights

- And Secondary Rights

Most of the top selling publications want to purchase *All Rights*, although many will settle for *First Rights*.

*All Rights* is what it sounds like; the publication buys all rights to what you wrote, and to use it as it seems fit. Sounds tough to take but what was really bought was the expression of the idea or topic and the editor can then make whatever editorial changes they want to in context with their publication.

They didn't buy the idea nor can they prevent you from using that idea somewhere else in a different fashion.

*First Rights* is better for you, because that very same article can be sold again and again without even changing one word. First rights allow the editor to use the article first, which means that it has never been used before in any other form.

This is something that you must adhere to, if only from a logistical standpoint, you can only sell this article to one editor at a time.

If an editor buys it and doesn't use it, what do you do?

You can't resell it until such time as the editor has returned your rights.

So by keeping track of the time since your submittal you could then go back to the editor and request this. You can still keep the money. You sold it in good faith; they just decided not to use it.

---

**Tip:** *Always write something that is worth stealing and then find an editor to buy it.*

---

## Taxes.

First a disclaimer.

If you are writing to earn income, you can also earn by saving at tax time.

This requires that you faithfully report your earnings, keep all of your receipts and records and be able to prove that these are business activities rather than a hobby.

So here is some general advice with regard to taxes. (You should seek specific advice from a tax accountant if necessary or even the IRS).

## • *Proof of Purchase.*

If you are writing to sell what you write and earn an income. And even doing that can be fun. All of your expenses attributable to writing are deductible.

*Proof of Purchase* is the key when challenged.

Two issues which are important when trying to demonstrate income earning intention. One is volume and the other is *"Letters of Intent"*.

You can prove volume by keeping a mailing record of every letter and manuscript sent to potential buyers.

In addition, retain copies of every manuscript or letter sent during that year. It goes without saying there should be a serious effort to show evidence of purpose in your writing activities. And the volume of items being offered for sale.

Sending out just one query per month will not justify deduct thousands of dollars in expenses. It will be denied.

## • *Letters of Intent.*

*Letters of Intent* are another important tax document. And sometimes it might be just the editor scribbling on the query itself "let's see it" or "Send on spec".

These are positive responses to your queries and thus you could deduct all reasonable expenses for going ahead and preparing that particular piece.

It isn't essential; that the editor buy the piece in order for you to deduct the expenses but, he needed to show some intent and you need that kind of documentation.

If the issue is ever questioned. It is just important that you have queried in a professional fashion and received a positive response and finally sent a piece for final consideration.

The key word here is reasonable. This is the definition of letter of intent. So hang onto and keep all such responses.

- ### *Track Those Expenses.*

You report your earning and expenses on Schedule C (Profit and Loss from Business and Profession) on the IRS 1040 Income Tax form. You may also need to submit Form 4562 (Depreciation and Amortization) and Schedule SE (Computation of Social Security Self-Employment Tax).

It just important that you keep a sensible track of your receipts spent on the money spent for writing.

When in doubt keep a record.

- The following is a list of items you should keep track of:

- Tips, coin phones and small change items (separate paper)

- Food costs on writing trips

- Car costs, per mile basis

- Necessary tools, Computers and Materials, Software programs

- Telephone for directly related purposes

- Cameras and tape recorders are depreciable

- Related supplies to camera and tape are deductible

- Travel costs and Entertainment related to writing

The key issue bears repeating, keep track of everything, even if you go on a trip and come back later and write.

Suppose you spend a year somewhere to learn about a new culture, well, if you come back later and put all those experiences into print, guess what? They're deductible.

The second you incur any expenses related to writing is the time you should start keeping track of your expenses and therefore can start taking deductions.

The IRS knows there is a certain amount of start-up costs going into a new business. And some of these expenses might add up for months or years before you start to make them payoff.

It takes some time to perfect your marketing and writing skills.

And in the meantime you've bought that computer, desk and bookshelves.

That won't last forever.

**A profit will certainly happen if you follow the guidelines addressed here in the *Over 65: Writing for Pleasure and Profit!* book!**

---

**Tip:** *You just can't have the expenses too far out of line in comparison to your income without bringing about some interest.*

---

Just be sensible, businesslike and you will be viewed as having a genuine purpose and not just approaching writing as a hobby. You can claim every deduction that is rightfully yours.

Any questions, again, you might need to consult a tax advisor.

# Chapter 11

## Converting the Process into Money and Reselling Your Work

*"We will either find a way, or make one."*
**-Hannibal, on crossing the Alps in 218 BC**

The *Over 65: Writing for Pleasure and Profit!* book asks the question:

## Once your article has been in print, why not sell it again and again?

It would make sense to put all that effort you put into research and rewrite it for another publication and market.

Professional writers do it all the time; it's perfectly legal and will dramatically *increase your income*!

So, if your article appeared in a magazine what's to stop you from putting the same material to work in a newspaper or book?

You might want to consider other geographic regions to sell your work to also.

## Reprints.

As we have discussed before reprints are *Second Right* sales.

Keep in mind that the term *Second Right* and *Reprint Rights* are the same. What it means is that a publication that bought your article on a first-rights basis, then it was printed, and you in turn, found another publication to sell it to.

As far as timing, you can sell the *Second Rights* the minute the First Rights publication hits the newsstands.

You don't have to ask for anybody permission because the editor that bought the first rights got what he paid for when he printed the article. That constituted your release from the first transaction.

*First Rights* means basically a one-time use, so that the rights automatically revert back to you when it was used.

*Second Rights* are simply a reprinting by anyone at any time, with your approval and their payment, of a piece of work that you've already done that's been in print.

You don't even have to change a word.

However, the only condition is that you need to inform the potential buyer of the *Second Rights* purchase, where the piece first appeared in print, the date of the publication, and that you are in fact offering second and reprint rights.

The best way to sell published seconds of an article is to cut and paste the published version of the article. Then send a copy to each possible buyer with a cover letter or note.

---

**Tip:** *You can even offer the piece to competing publications.*

---

Making sure that if one buys it that you don't sell it to another with any intentions of exclusivity. You want to be able to approach these editors in the future or they might have a topic they want you to write about which is similar and you just don't want to get them mad at you and cost future sales.

## The cover letter is the most important part of reselling a reprint.

The letter has to be a tease to get the editor to read the actual work, so it needs to be good. No one in their right mind will read a paste up unless the letter sounds irresistible.

Also, remember if you had additional materials-photos, slides, illustrations, charts-that weren't used be the first publication, you could offer these now to enhance the prospects of the sale.

In your cover letter, offer to send the original work, typed-double spaced, perhaps with a compatible word file (ask for the correct program the publication uses, Word, Adobe, etc.) to facilitate typesetting and production.

Most users in this category will pay upon publication and this helps you identify those that are actually going to be users.

Why else would they request the original?

Finally, don't forget to include a SASE!

## Rewrites.

### This is simply the original article rewritten.

They in effect are new articles, different and can be sound like any other article, all-rights, first-rights, and simultaneous submissions and so on.

A *Rewrite* will likely use some or all the information gathered doing the research for the first article, only it will be now written to have an identity of its own.

*Rewrites* are typically done when you have sold all the rights to an original article and you now want to put a different angle on it and generate more sales from the research.

---

**Tip:** *The editor is only buying the rights to the copy not the idea, so you can go ahead and use the idea in many different ways and forms, whatever it takes to generate more sales and maximize the benefit of the time that went into your research.*

---

In this context, of course there should be significant difference in the lead, the body of the piece and the conclusion.

A new title is a given.

But using previous quotes and anecdotes is certainly allowable and will help to spice up the piece, besides they worked in the original article why not use them again? Again you are looking at the topic from a different angle.

## Modified Reprints.

Some reprints require some rewriting in order for them to make the piece acceptable. (Like what I'm doing for this book?)

A *modified reprint* if sufficiently altered to create another piece, has all the credibility of a rewrite.

And there's no reason that it can't be sold to a publication as a distinctly new piece, on a *first-rights* basis, then later resold as a reprint once it has appeared in print.

It's a reprint of a rewrite.

And a modified rewrite is a new manuscript with its own rights!

## Make the Big Money.

If you really want to make big money by writing, you need to follow the process that has been outlined in this book and add a major new element at the beginning now that will multiply your research yield.

You need to expedite the querying and preparation, and put the maximum number of pieces in print in the least amount of time.

For the lack of a better name we here at the *Over 65: Writing for Pleasure and Profit!* book call it:

## "Subject Rippling".

*Subject rippling* differs from the process we have been advocating up until this point.

In subject rippling you take your idea or topic and rather than just write one article from it, use it as the basis for as many related articles, all of which draw for the original feasibility study done to create a reference source bank.

The concept comes from the rippling appearance of the article ideas coming from the initial subject idea of information.

The concept will be explained by way of an analogy:

*Think of a sailboat (the idea/topic) moving along on top of the water, as it moves, triangulating out from its path is a series of primary, and then secondary waves, resulting from the initial path of the sailboat.*

'*Subject rippling*' requires a deviation in timing and on the explanation of the risk involved with the standard approach:

Query – write –sell – resell - rewrite process.

Both take the idea of the original topic (sailboat) and create new ideas, as your energy and the potential readership interests' dictates.

As one idea is investigated before querying, so are the rest.

The wider the research expands, guess what? The more articles and topic ideas will emerge.

## The key here is the savings in time.

This approach will allow you to extract articles faster and easier, and gather basic querying information about as many subjects with the same base topic, than to return to that material each time you want to explore the many related ideas.

This approach saves time, as it will in the long run, be more efficient to compile an extended source list of items in print about a particular subject.

Putting together a few more solid hours working on the bibliography, from which the information for the articles are drawn upon will later make it far simpler to write the related or "*rippled*" articles.

The only risk here is that you might spent too much time here developing the subject rippling program, and not enough query writing that would justify the sales or time.

**The reward with this new approach far outweigh the risks.**

Since writing query letters contain only a few paragraphs of anecdotes, facts and quotes, selecting from a larger bank of information will allow you to multiply the potential sales from your efforts.

With the one idea-one sale approach, you have spent a considerable amount of time at the feasibility, query and research writing stages just to receive a few hundred dollars from the sale.

Even with the reprints and rewrites, the per hour earnings ratio makes freelance writing a highly skilled, low paying disciplined. Any good material discovered by your research is often times abandoned in the search for another query or sale.

But, you want to be a professional writer, you want to paint this picture a little differently, that's why you are reading this book (n'est-ce pas?).

As you become more familiar with the selling process and use the same research more than once, heck, it's easier than going back out to the library or doing all that research again on the internet. Isn't it?

Beginners are typically afraid to go back and reuse the same information. Somehow they are misguided by what they think the laws are or copyrights or through their own ignorance.

***Subject rippling* is not only permissible; it is the best of all possible paths to follow from an overall fiscal standpoint if you want to make your living as a writer.**

---

**Tip:** *The key here is that once you have sold an idea, "subject ripple" it and take that $350 sale and turn it into $1000, $2000 or more with the rippled ideas.*

---

Seems like a lot to do at first if you are new to writing.

Your head aches and your hand shakes at the thought of going through all of this while so much is at risk.

If you are new to writing it always is going to feel more comfortable to concentrate on making that first sale then on to making reprints and rewrites.

You in fact, need to learn by doing every facet of this process.

But then go back, looking at it from the perspective of *Subject Rippling* and that original strong idea will have others right within it which will equally as strong.

Use the first sale as the basis for your *Subject-Rippling*, but apply the steps you took on a faster and more efficient way.

Indeed *Subject-Rippling* can be done after the initial sale, though it makes the most sense to do it doing the feasibility phase. So if this has been your approach you can return to those that have sold and *Subject-Ripple* them to gather up lost sales.

## Let's point out the steps and advantages of "Subject Rippling":

(1)  Expand the original idea.

(2)  Query magazine, write, reprint, rewrite.

(3)  Simultaneous submissions.

(4)  Look from alternative angles or spins on the idea that sells.

(5)  Planning and research of additional ideas.

(6)  As the number of ripples grow out from the original subject so does your resource list.

(7)  Extended research leads to how much has already been printed about a subject and to create new ripples of ideas for new articles related to the original idea.

(8) This additional research will make it essay to compile new facts, quotes and anecdotes for the other query letters.

(9) Now that you have the ripples, you need to decide how to market them.

(10) As before, you develop a market list or lists and query the top publications(s).

(11) Continue this process for each ripple in the process, under each ripple see how ways you can come up with for how the topic can be marketed, query, simultaneous submission, etc.

(12) Now draw from the bank of resource you have develop from your feasibility study.

(13) Respond to those queries that have received a positive response.

(14) Look to avoid overall and yet look for the greatest market penetration.

(15) Now you got a real sales plan for your efforts, yes it took a little bit longer but think of the rewards.

(16) Instead now you lay out your entire marketing program for many ideas at the same time, and rather that flood just one market with many queries and submissions, you mold the subject to suit as many different markets as possible.

This is the approach to taking a $300 one shot idea and turning it into a $3000 one subject topic in far less time than it would take to make ten one-shot sales.

## Try it!

You'll like the results, there's no magic to it.

**It's the best way to make more money writing with this *Over 65: Writing for Pleasure and Profit!* book approach!**

# *Chapter 12*

## Writing for a Specific Industry and Marketing Yourself as a Writer

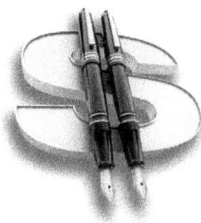

*"It takes nearly as much ability
to know how to profit by good advice,
As to know how to act for one's self."*
**-Francois de la Rochefoucauld**

The *Over 65: Writing for Pleasure and Profit!* book has tried to show you how you can sell an idea in article form to magazines and newspapers.

In addition, this book has outlined the process for researching and targeting specific markets, whether it be magazine, newspaper, book or the film industry.

Many of the examples highlighted in the *Over 65: Writing for Pleasure and Profit!* book has been tailored to round out the selling process.

Hopefully, you have come this far and understand more about your career as a writer and the rationale and format for producing marketable copy.

This lesson is focused on writing for specific industries, with an elaboration of format and procedures.

In addition, we conclude our work with an outline of a potential marketing plan that you might want to consider as a guideline for your own over 65 writing career.

Included with the marketing plan are some "do's" and "don'ts" about marketing, a discussion about self-publishing, and some additional resources available to you as a professional writer from The *Over 65: Writing for Pleasure and Profit!* book.

## Writing for Specific Industries.

The order of this chapters' discussion will be as follows:

- Magazines

- Newspapers

- Books

- On-Line Publications (Blogs, eJournals and ebooks, etc.)

## Magazines.

You could increase your income by including sidebars.

This works equally well for magazines or newspapers. For the magazine market, you typically mentioned the possible creation of a sidebar near the end of the query letter and go ahead and write it if the editor shows some interest. This would be submitted with the article text in the same double-spaced format.

For the newspaper market, you would typically write both the main article and the sidebar and send them together, usually simultaneously to as many editors that you have researched who represent non-competing markets.

At the top of the piece, you need to identify it as the "SIDEBAR" or "BOX".

Both terms mean the same thing, and the reason is just that you don't want the editor to confuse it with the larger article it is accompanied.

## Magazine Slide Caption Sheets.

Most publications that purchase artwork from freelancers prefer color slides.

And if you have any to go along with your piece these should be mentioned in the query letter. If the editor expresses any interest in seeing them and you would then send them with the completed work, unless the editors asks you to do it differently.

Each slide should be labeled and sent in a thick, clear plastic holder.

If sent by a digital jpeg, tif, etc. version, you should clearly identify the file name and each individual image name, coordinating the location in the piece by a numerical code reference, or another easily trackable system.

Most editors will need an explanation of every slide, detailing how you think it might be used with the piece or why it should be considered. Make sure you also include your name and how you can be contacted.

## Newspaper Articles.

Some observations about writing specifically for the newspaper market:

(1)   Don't make your pieces too long.

For example, the travel section generally only has one main article written by the editor himself and then several shorter pieces. Roughly from about 1000 to 1600 words in length.

(2)   Don't include a specific title that has to be used.

Newspapers have tight space demands so that will typically create their own title. Perhaps the only deviation from this would be a humor piece where changing the title might not match the context or style of the article. It which case, this title should be as short as possible.

(3)   You might want to insert sub-headings where appropriate, particularly if the article is regional or divided into some natural boundary.

(4)   Always include your byline, who the work was written by, and one sentence about you and your experience under the title so the editor knows who to send the check to.

(5)   And on every page, even though you don't see it here, (you won't even have to think about this, as you become more experienced), set up a typical page header format, which includes your name, address and phone/fax information.

## Newspaper Photos.

Typically, newspapers will buy black and white photographs to accompany the major key articles. In your cover letter attached to the completed work, you should mention the availability of B/W's, which would be forwarded if the article is purchased.

Usually five images are enough, and you should tell the editor that you have the proofs and will send suggestions for the captions to accompany each photo.

Again, make sure to include your name, address, and phone/fax, plus a SASE which will assist the editors with a prompt request of the negatives from you.

## The Newspaper Follow-up.

You really don't need to go out of your way here, but a brief follow-up note to the editor, just to thank them for using your article and to keep your name in front of them.

---

**Tip:** *You would like to write for them again, editors who have purchased your work once, are more than likely to keep buying from you, without as much effort, as long as the quality of your writing stays the same and matches the expectations and promises that you make in each query.*

---

Just keep the follow-up note simple.

## Book Query Follow-up Letter.

Not every book query results in a book.

But you need to maintain a working relationship with all the book editors you contacted and sent the original query even though it didn't pan out.

Why?

You open up the possibility for a future book about a better topic and you haven't burned your bridges. And a bridge unburned is one you can cross in the future.

## Self-Publishing.

Many authors like to take control of their own destiny and self-publish their own work. But keep in mind, that self-publishing isn't for every person or every book.

Keep in mind, a Nonfiction book may be difficult to publish independently unless it fills in a particular niche.

## With that lies the secret.

You need to have a narrowly focused topic to reach a particular market.

For example, a book about "saxophone training" or "mouthpieces", for example, is better than one just about musical instruments, because you can find a target audience.

In this example, school music programs, retail music stores, saxophone journal/musical magazine mailing lists, conferences, jazz festivals, are all rich hunting grounds. Perhaps you can merchandise the book to a saxophone manufacturer, etc.

To prosper in the self-publishing you must have certain characteristics:

- Being a writer is only the beginning.

- Marketing is crucial.

- You must be willing to acquire this knowledge or hire someone who possesses it.

- Self-discipline is important because you will be wearing many different hats.

- A self-publisher is a writer, editor, book designer, type setter, printer, business manager, bookkeeper, order fulfiller and publicist. Typically you'll subcontract a lot of these functions.

But ultimately, it's your project, and – you not only create the design, but you make sure it gets built the way you envisioned it - you are also the "construction superintendent".

## It takes time, money and energy.

Here you need to make sure your motivation is clear.

The self-publishing option is undertaken because the self-publisher wants to make a profit. Done properly, this approach can be very lucrative.

Done improperly, you can lose your shirt.

You can make a whopping 80% on your book, but you are going to work hard for it.

---

**Tip:** *If you are the person who likes to get behind The wheel, rather than just go for the ride, self-publishing is the perfect alternative for getting your book in print.*

---

Perhaps your goal is to influence people about a subject you feel strongly about or have a particular viewpoint. Many professionals seek to position themselves as 'experts'. A book gives them new forms of visibility and credibility.

## When you elect to self-publish you are going into business, so do your homework.

Learn about printing, it'll be your biggest expense. To be cost effective, we are talking about 2000 to 3000 copies of most books and you'll need to work with a book manufacturer or print broker to get the best deal.

Other options are "print-on-demand" (POD) companies, such as Lulu.com, Createspace.com, etc., which reduce the author risk by printing and mailing ordered copies.

The efficiencies of these companies far aweigh the aggravation and expense of being the middle man yourself and handling all the order filling, packaging and mailing.

Keep in mind, these companies make their margins and your royalties are lower, but with significant sales it can be a very viable option.

These two, Createspace and Lulu offer direct distribution agreements and marketing services with Amazon and other online retailers.

Below is an example from the cover of a 400-page (POD) self published book (Media Tipping Points):

### Media Tipping Points

This Printed On Demand (POD) book addresses three comparative case studies in which the concept of the Tipping Point is evidenced during global events that are in many ways influenced by the media. The case studies were selected on the basis of (3) common key attributes: contagiousness, stickiness (during their development), and one dramatic moment in time that could be defined as a Tipping Point.

These case studies were also chosen largely because their attributes included the (4) characteristics of people, organizations, media and events that could be categorically analyzed and compared within a conceptual framework, including recent events that were impacted by global media. The case studies are about the literature, trends, and information relative to media impact on global events in the context of the Tipping Point phenomenon, which are interpreted in the context of much broader event themes. These case studies represent only a few of the global events that meet the criteria for the Tipping Point Theory Analysis: Media Impact on Global Events.

The first case study, the presidential campaign of Barack Obama, was chosen in order to examine a narrower scope and timeframe for the analysis with a finite endpoint, and also because geographically, politically, economically, and culturally, only one nation is involved. In contrast, the second case study, the financial crisis of 2007 through 2010, involves more complex issues that impact other nation states and global economies. It requires an analysis on a much broader scale in time, 2007 to the present, with origins centered primarily in one country, yet in contrast to the first study, represented a larger field of data and information to analyze.

The last case study, climate change, is included because, although the two first case studies provide a basis for understanding critical tipping point attributes and their characteristics, with its ongoing nature, it presents probable solutions and parameters for analyzing how tipping actually evolves and what its subsequent impact on a global scale could be. The climate change case study involves many nation states and many complex contemporary media development issues and technology changes integral to the research that is continuing to evolve. The correlations between these global events and media impact exhibited very strong cause and effect relationships between the tipping point attributes and the case study evolutions.

The case studies were also selected to be examined in this book on the basis of quantity and accessibility of information about the attributes and characteristics, their history in the context of media and impact, and emergence of a model theory framework to apply to future global events.

These three case studies encompass relevant examples with regard to media impact and global events. They offer considerable variety in terms of their geographic locations as well as their scale, historical, social and political context, and consequently, they lend themselves to comparisons that exhibit these similarities and differences. In the course of comparing and analyzing them, consideration is given to the subdominant questions of why media has such an impact on global events, and why we have not already embraced the model for the purposes of addressing climate change. Throughout this book, many of the interpretations of the material are my own unless otherwise specified.

References in the case studies are identified in alphabetical order so as to present a neutral and consistent way of referring to the sources in this context and therefore not implying any political or personal biases based on the order in which the references are named. Similarly, the text and information reproduced in the annexes are done alphabetically first, as they do not necessarily illustrate the timeline continuity of the events as they unfold during the case studies.

Other events in retrospect might have been chosen, such as the recent events involving Tunisia, Egypt, Libya, Bahrain, and other countries in the Arab region. But due to time constraints and limited knowledge of the culture and language, these and other more recent events were dismissed.

## Marketing Yourself as a Writer

The following are some tips on self promotion as a writer:

- One of the best ways to build a writing career is to find a niche, market it and create it to sell your work.

- Don't be afraid to promote yourself and your work.

- Always keep in mind that your goals are to increase your visibility, build your career, and achieve success.

- Give readings of your work.

- Arrange lecturing and speaking gigs. Use a lecture agent or do it on your own.

- Have business cards printed up. Give them to anyone who might conceivably use your services. Including every editor or producer who has accepted your work.

- Have a publication or production party; invite friends, writers and people you would like to meet.

- Send out new copies of your book to reviewers and editors, anybody that you think might help you.

- Seek endorsements from other writers and personalities.

## Promote yourself in the media as someone worth interviewing and writing about.

### Send out news releases.

Particularity those organizations that do interviews of writers and reviews of books.

Never push your friends or family to help you in your promotional efforts or even to buy your work.

Do invite them to events and functions, and accept their help if they offer it freely.

## How Much Should You Charge?

To do the best you can financially as a writer, you need to be talented and immensely creative.

This book has pointed out the literally thousands and thousands of markets for the written word.

While the on-line publications and magazine markets are the prime markets for starting your career, there are other markets that serve as significant money making alternatives.

Before deciding how much you should charge for a particular work, you should always read samples of other pieces in the specific publications and refer to the writer guidelines that you have previously requested from each.

## Now when you start to set your fees, you should keep the following factors in consideration:

- Pay rates in your area, niche or expertise.

- Amount of Competition.

- How much you think the client is willing or able to pay for the work.

- How much you want to earn for your time and effort.

One approach might be to figure out what you want to make in a given year, and divide that by the number of hours per week, per year.

This way you can arrive at an hourly rate to charge. (Don't forget to include overhead, expenses, meetings, insurance, vacations, retirement, hospitalization, etc).

---

**Tip:** *Another way is to refer to the Writer's Digest for the complete listing of writing categories and pay ranges for each. (Bear in mind, this is just a reference and actual rates can vary widely).*

---

Regardless of the method by which you arrive at your fee for the job, just make sure you get a letter of agreement signed by both parties covering the work to be done and the fee to be paid.

If there is any question about the how long the project will take you, be sure you include an estimate of how many hours your fee is based on and if more time is required you then need to re negotiate with the client.

Some clients pay hourly rates and some clients pay a flat fee for jobs, and sometimes you think you are giving your services away just to get in the door.

**But keep in mind that you are building your portfolio, getting experience and more print visibility.**

Good luck and let us know about your success!

**Thanks for reading:**
**The *Over 60: Writing for Pleasure and Profit!* book!**

# References and Resources

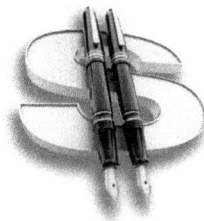

## References and Resources

*AllReaders.com* (http://www.allreaders.com) is a web site that allows for look up of books and their authors by searching on plot lines and other elements. This might prove useful if you are seeking a particular author or book.

*The Art of Writing Webzine* (http://www.artofwritingzine.com) is an ezine for and about writers with areas on vocabulary, resources and instructional how to's.

*Black and White* (http://www.bfree.on.ca/bow) is an interesting concept. A set of contracts that you can sign promising to complete so much writing and if you do not check back with your results you can invite other Black and White members to prompt you to get going.

*American Name Society Homepage* (http://ssie.binghamton.edu/admin/anshomep.html) highlights a society that is dedicated to the study of names and naming practices. The site includes information about a mailing list.

*Art Resources* (http://custwww.xensei.com/adl/ar) is a broad range of links to resources relating to all parts of the artistic community, including some links to writing resources specifically.

*Britannica.com* (http://www.brittannica.com) is the revamped online presence of Britannica Encyclopedia. Hands down this is far and away the best encyclopedia on the planet and their web site is a huge comprehensive center for research and exploration. From Arts to the World, the subject area are comprehensive, interesting and fun to explore. This is a must see site and about the only down side may be that its own popularity has overwhelmed their server initially and may do so again. Simply put, check it out.

*The Burry Man* (http://www.burryman.com) is a resource for writers that cover a diverse number of areas. Well worth a look.

*The Classics Archive* http://the-tech.mit.edu/Classics) has an archive of hundreds of translated Classic texts including the Aenid, the Odyssey and others.

*C/NET's Search.com* (http://www.search.com) is an impressive archive of search resources on the internet.

*CybRpunk* (http://w3.one.net/~wronk/cybrpunk.html) is a page devoted to the Cyperpunk genre.

*emilyv.com* (http://www.emilyv.com/index.htm) or, more descriptively, *Writing for the Web* is a general writing site with a focus. This sites focus is helping professional writers promote, publish, and sell their writing on the Web. The site includes both free resources and some commercial items such as What Every Writer Must Know About E-Publishing Overall, well worth a visit.

*Encyclopedia.com* (http://www.encyclopedia.com) is a useful online encyclopedia sponsored by Electric Library with over 17,000 short listings to a keyword search.

*Encyclopedia Mythica* (http://www.pantheon.org) is an interesting compendium of information relating to mythology and other info that might be of use in writing historical fiction, fantasy or even certain science fiction such as Lord of Light.

*Fiction Rag: A Web Site About Writers and Writing* (http://www.syx.com/rag) is just as it sounds, a reflective and pleasant look at the writers life as seen through the eyes of Martha Conway.

*fictionsearch.com* (http://www.fictionsearch.com) is an extensive database of a wide ranging grouping of topics related to the interests of both the writing and reading community. It is well worth a look.

*Forward Motion: Holly Lisle's Writing Pages* (http://www.sff.net/people/holly.lisle) grew out of her print newsletter related to writing. It includes many of the articles that started life there including 'How To Quit Your

Day Job' and many more. It also has a wealth of links, a mailing list and much more. Well worth a look.

***The FBI Freedom of Information Site*** (http://foia.fbi.gov) is a wealth of information about criminals and more and links to other sites of diverse content. Whether you are interested in Al Capone or fingerprinting or what have you, this is one place to possibly look.

***Garbl's Writing Resources*** (http://garbl.home.comcast.net) has a number of interesting links to resources and to a variety of experts online that might be of assistance. Some of the experts are commercial services, but if there is need for their services this is one spot to check for them.

***Haiku for People*** (http://www.oslonett.no/home/keitoy/haiku.html) is a site where you learn all about Haiku and how to write Haiku poems as well.

***Hatch's Plot Bank*** (http://www.angelfire.com/nc/tcrpress/plotbank.html) is almost precisely want it sounds like, 2000+ one line plot ideas and growing. If you want a place to just go and peruse and get random inspiration this possible could be the spot for you.

***The Helio-Centric Network*** (http://www.wolfe.net/~lbothell) or Three Stones Publications, Ltd. Homepage, has a wealth of interesting links well worth a visit.

***HollywoodNet*** (http://www.hollywoodnetwork.com) has a variety of resources related to screenwriting, acting, directing and producing.

***The Holy See*** (http://www.vatican.va) is just what it sounds like, the Vatican's website. Worth a visit if nothing else to explore the archive of documents that have been made available.

***How to Research Architecture*** (http://www.nypl.org/research/chss/spe/art/artarc/archit/Arch.html) is precisely as it sounds and is sponsored by the New York City Library on top of it. This is not just a list of links, but strategies for how to go about researching the style, history and so on of a building or buildings. If you are interested in adding complexity, scope and place to your writings this is an important set of tools to acquire.

*Itools* (http://www.itools.com) is an interesting compendium of search engines and research tools that should be useful in nailing down details and searching for added detail.

*The Jewish Heritage Online Magazine* (http://www.jewishheritage.com/index.html) is one place to go for details of Jewish history, the Jewish calendar and much more.

*Linguistics Sources on the World-Wide-Web* (http://gpu2.srv.ualberta.ca/~slis/guides/linguist/ling2.htm) is a good place to look for information on the scholarly side of linguistics.

*Legends* (http://www.legends.dm.net/) is a marvelous site that concentrates on the legends that haunt our stories and literature and the historical background for each. There are a wealth of links and a lot to interest a writer here. So much so that it is linked both from general writer resources and historical references. If you are interested in Arthur, Robin Hoo, pirates and much more this is the place to go.

*Library Spot* (http://www.libraryspot.com) is one stop shopping for a variety of library resources with links to all manner of libraries including law, medical and musical and much more.

*The Library of Congress* (http://www.loc.gov) has a range of links that could prove useful as a place to look for information. This is only to be expected since it is the Library of Congress.

*Literary Kicks* (http://www.charm.net/~brooklyn/LitKicks.html) is self explanatory and also was a GNN Best of the Web nominee some years back. If you want to find out about Jack Kerovac, Allen Ginsberg and the whole beat phenomena, this is the place to go. Its worth going just for its own sake.

***Liszt - the mailing list directory*** (http://www.liszt.com) is a comprehensive compendium of mailing lists broken up into a variety of different subject areas. If you want to join a community of other knowledgable inidividuals or not so knowledgable individuals as the case may be to explore an area of interest this may be the site to visit.

***The Mining Co.'s Writers Exchange*** (http://writerexchange.miningco.com) is an excellent site for a whole array of links of interest for writers.

***Misc.Writing Homepage*** (http://www.scalar.com/mw) is the website for the usenet newsgroup that concentrates on this wonderful artform of writing.

***The Mosaic Magazine Archives*** (http://www.nasw.org/users/mosaic/index.html) is a searchable index of science articles generated in that magazine between 1970-1992. Be warned that there is a charge for delivery of the articles.

***Myths and Legends*** (http://pubpages.unh.edu/~cbsiren/myth.html) covers a wide variety of cultures and their myths and legends.

***My Virtual Reference Desk*** (http://www.refdesk.com) is a must visit site with a a vaste array of links to newspaper, map sites, dictionaries, thesauruses and more.

***The National Academy Press*** (http://www.nap.edu) is a bookstore, but it also has a wealth of resources and links useful for those interested in science.

***The National Assembly of State Art Agencies*** (http://www.nasaa-arts.org) might prove useful.

***Novel Advice*** (http://www.noveladvice.com) is an electronic newsletter for writers with advice from writers and seeks submissions. Its focus is the craft of writing. It also has online invitation only critique groups that you can enquire about from their site.

**One Women's Writing Retreat** (http://www.prairieden.com) is a wide ranging attempt at a writing community with a chat area, guestbook page and a wealth of links. You might want to click on the Sitemap to get to a nicely laid out division of resources.

**The OnLine English 'phrase-checker'** (http://www.oleng.com.au/indexpc.html) puts together search engine technology to support writers of English. In its own words 'It provides a window to a FAST search for the exact phras'. When, for example, scientists preparing journal articles are unsure if particular phrases can be used or how they can be used, the phrase checker provides links to multiple, real-world examples of any English phrase in context'. This looks to have possible uses over many more standard search engines.

**Odin's Castle of Dreams and Legends** (http://www.wf.net/~odin/index.html) is a massive site with a wide range of interesting links for random or focused research that can be as long ago as the mists of the prehistoric to modern times.

**Poets and Writers Online** (http://www.pw.org) is a tremendous resource with many resource links and opportunities for networking. Well worth a look.

**Preditors and Editors** (http://www.anotherealm.com/prededitors) has a wealth of links to potential markets and services for writers.

**Prelude.net** (http://www.prelude.net) is a beginning writing resource that hopes to have the elements for fostering a writing community. These include writers forums and links and more. It does have a business side in that it is offering hosting services for webzines. The prices for domain accounts are reasonable on the face of them. Overall, this site has possibilities and will certainly grow.

**Project Gutenberg** (http://promo.net/pg) is an excellent resource for searching for the actual text of a whole host of different manuscripts from the past. This site is not strictly historical in nature and as such deserves listing in several categories at forwriters.com. So it is that it located both here in general resources and in historical sites.

**Publicly Accessible Mailing Lists** (http://www.neosoft.com/internet/paml) is a searchable index of the same that is ideal for a variety of research endeavors. Mailing lists are becoming a definite alternative to the overload of newsgroups. Well worth checking out.

**Pure Fiction** (http://www.purefiction.com) has its focus in the best selling novel and how to write one. The site has a wealth of resources worth a look at. Of special interest for any and all interested in using the internet for research there is the Internet Research FAQ (http://www.purefiction.com/pages/res1.htm).

**Rest Stop Online Newsletter for Writers** (http://www.geocities.com/SoHo/Village/2115/index.html) is an outgrowth of the Rest Stop Writer's Forum on Delphi. This is a quite useful resource for information on a broad range of questions in regard to writing. Check it out.

**The Science Fiction and Fantasy Writers of America, Inc.** (http://www.sfwa.org/) is a vital resource as an organization and equally good resource as a homepage. Among its many other resources including style guides and other resources there is the Warnings and Cautions for Writers (http://www.sfwa.org/Beware/Warnings.html).

The Screenwriters/Playwrights Page (http://www.teleport.com/ ~cdeemer/scrwriter.html) is a longstanding resource that concentrates on the needs of the Screenwriter and Playwright.

**The SFWA Writers Beware Page** (http://www.sfwa.org/Beware) is an excellent resource for many cautionary suggestions you might want to take into account before getting yourself into trouble.

**SharpWriters.com** (http://www.sharpwriter.com) is a general writing resource that spawned from the Clocktower Fiction site. An excellent resource including encyclopedias, punctuation and a whole range of others.

**A Sociological Tour Through Cyberspace** (http://www.trinity.edu/~mkearl/index.html) is a compendium of all things sociological and well worth an exploration.

If you don't have a copy of the Bard just laying around you can check the complete works of **Shakespeare** (http://the-tech.mit.edu/Shakespeare/works.html) available on the internet.

**Stumper-L** (http://www.cuis.edu/~stumpers/intro.html) is where you can get subscribed to be on the mailing list for reference librarians where things that have got them stumped can be answered.

**Tips for Writers** (http://www.tipsforwriters.com) is in its own description 'Resources, links, articles, and references designed to help you build your writing career and get published!' It is all that and more. Well worth a visit.

**TrainWeb** (http://trainweb.com) is where to go for information about anything to do with trains from freight and passenger trains to model railroads.

**The UniGuide Academic Guide to the Internet** (http://www.aldea.com/guides/ag/attframes2.html) has a wealth of resources that are all tested for authenticity. Well worth a look around.

**The U.S. Census Bureau** (http://www.census.gov) is an extensive site with many research resources, but many of which require a fee.

**Voice of the Shuttle** (http://vos.ucsb.edu) is a unique resources with a wealth of links and emphasis on being a resource for humanities research.

**The WWW Bible Gateway** (http://www.gospelcom.net/bible) is a useful resource for those searching for bible quotes. You can look particular passages or search by subject.

**The Victory Page** (http://www.webcom.com/~victory) has links to writer resources, a motivational newsletter, workshops for novelists and other interesting features.

**Web Assisted Self Publishing** (http://www.hkbu.edu.hk/~ppp/WASP.html) is a good place to check out on this burdgeoning field.

*The Web Writer* (http://www.geocities.com/Athens/Parthenon/8390) is an inevitable resource. A New York based site intent on advising people on how best to write for the web as opposed to any other medium. Interesting and well worth a look.

*Where To For Writers* (http://www.writead.com/homesearch.htm) is a general index of interesting sites including topical areas such as where to read great fiction, where to submit your work, where to improve your writing and where to find resources.

*Wikipedia* (http://en.wikipedia.org/wiki/Main_Page) is perhaps the reference site for the whole web as the one and only free encyclopedia that is perpetually updated by the services of those who visit the site. This is a must visit for anyone who wants to peruse an idea and expand on it for a story or essay or whatever else.

*Word Play* (http://www.wordplayer.com) is a resource for those interested in Screenplays with a variety of forums to share ideas and thoughts about this area of writing.

*The Word Wizard* (http://wordwizard.com) is a free resource that looks to have some potential.

*@Writers* (http://www.geocities.com/Athens/Acropolis/6608/) has a chat area and an email newsletter.

*Writer's BBS* (http://www.writersbbs.com) has a lot of chatrooms and discussions areas related to writing, readers and other areas of artistic endeavor.

*Writer's Block* (http://www.niva.com/writblok) is an online Writer's Magazine that has a wealth of interesting articles and features as well as a an aesthetically pleasing look.

*Writer's Block* (http://sff.net/people/LisaRC) is Lisa R. Cohen's page devoted to the trials and tribulation of Writer's Block and the advice on getting out of it.

*The Write Resource* (http://www.write-resource.com) is a general writers resource along the lines of forwriters.com. In their own words they describe themselves as "We have hundreds of resource links as well as terms, quotes, downloads, calendars and more!" Worth a look.

*Writers Forum* (http://www.homestead.com/pressassociation/forum.html) is an online resource for writers provided by Phil Philcox and the Press Association Staff. Well worth a look and perusal for tips, tricks and possible ideas.

*Writer's Home* (http://www.writershome.com) is a robust and comprehensive web site with many resources open for your use as a freelance writer, including an Editors Only Site, a place to post your resume and more. Well worth a look.

*The Writers Gallery* (http://www.onestep.com/writers) is just as described, a gallery of examples of various writing from novels to poetry even including haiku.

*Gail and Pete Robertson's Writers' Information Registry* (http://www.pacificcoast.net/~gprobert/registry.html) is an appealing and perhaps unique concept. The site is a registry of people who have agreed to be contact persons for places, activities or life experiences. As they note, 'We cannot verify the information provided to requesters by participants, nor guarantee that participants are as they have depicted themselves'. Still, this looks like a truly invaluable resource for those seeking to do research in an area.

*The Writers Link Center* (http://www.writerswebsite.com) has a wide range of links covering everything from Communication as in forums and bulletin boards to Written By, where you can link your articles, stories or whatever directly to their site. An interesting and potentially useful site.

*The Writer's Mirror* (http://www.manninweb.co.im/writer/wmirror.html) is an online zine for writers with articles, resource links and reviews as well as an email newsletter. UK based, it also includes workshops in the local area. Worth look and consideration as a possible home for articles that help writers write.

*The Writer's Place* (http://www.awoc.com/AWOC-Home.cfm) website has an online searchable database of publisher submission guidelines for over 400 publishers, a free ezine (Writing for Dollars), and more.

*Writers Resource Center* (http://www.comet.chv.va.us/writersr/index1.htm) has a wealth of links nicely categorized and quite functional. Of particular interest is the historical research page, but it has other links to a broad range of subjects as well.

*Writer's Resources* (http://www.arcana.com/shannon/writing.html) has a wealth of interesting links from specifics to general.

*Writers Web* (http://www.homestead.com/writers_links/authorlink.html) is a site for link entries including electronic self publication, author web sites and other possible inclusions. At this posting all of the links appear to be self publication. However, as times goes along, others should be included here.

*The Writers Workshop* (http://www.scifi-az.com/sfaz-05.htm) area of Michael McCollum's Sci Fi Arizona is an excellent archive of articles of interest to writers. Of particular interest is Acrobat PDF version of Practical Astrogation For Science Fiction Writers. For those that want to know what stars are within 50 lights years of Earth, this is invaluable.

*writing-world.com* (http://www.writing-world.com) is a successor to the for inkling newsletter and Inkspot web site. It includes may resource links and a twice weekly email newsletter.

*The WWW Bible Gateway* (http://www.gospelcom.net/bible) is a useful resource for those searching for bible quotes. You can look particular passages or search by subject. Writing Now (http://www.writingnow.com) is an ezine dedicated to helping writers market their works.

*Zuzu's Petals Literary Links* (http://www.zuzu.com/poelink.htm) has a wealth of links relating to everything from Poetry to fiction.

## Writing for Comics

*Marc Fleury's Writing for Comics* (http://www.geocities.com/Athens/ Forum/9925/") is an excellent resource for researching the state of the market, how to write the scripts and all else related to this industry.

## The Business of Writing

*Cyn Mason* has produced an excellent essay on Taxes for Writers. A copy of this is now available here on forwriters.com both in an HTML version (http://www.forwriters.com/taxes.html) and a Word document file (http://www.forwriters.com/Taxes.doc). This is appropriate for writers paying US taxes.

For anyone desiring information about copyrights here is a *Copyright and Intellectual Properties Resource* (http://www.nlc-bnc.ca/ifla/II/ cpyright.htm) and the more a writer can learn about copyrights the better.

Another site of interest about this is the *Copyright Website* (http://www. benedict.com).

*The Cybarrister's Page* (http://www.ssbb.com/cybarr.html) is an interesting place to explore some of the legal ramification of the cyberspace/electronic media.

*A Guide to Copyrights* (http://www.ior.com/~malhotra/copy.html) is a simply well layed out question and answer faq style analysis of this important issue for writers.

*The U.S. Copyright Office's Gopher site* (gopher://marvel.loc.gov/11/ copyright) is a somewhat more primitive interface for those new to the web, but has a variety of interesting and useful information online.

*Lars Eighner's Writer's Index Page* (http://www.io.com/~eighner/ wrtrmain.html) includes a checklist of common mistakes that writers make when doing submissions as well as online courses in writing.

*The Publishing Law Center* (http://www.publaw.com) is just as it sounds. Provided by the Law Office of Lloyd L. Rich, it covers a wealth of areas with articles relating to the legal consideration of getting published. They are quick to point out that this is not legal advice, because individual circumstances can range widely. However, this could be a useful and interesting site to visit.

*The Twenty Writing Tools* (http://www.geocities.com/RodeoDrive/2385/writing_tools.html) are basic rules of thumbs for a writer that most should know but might be useful for others.

For those interested in what are the bestsellers try *USA Today's Bestsellers 1-50* (http://www.usatoday.com/life/enter/books/leb1.htm) and *Bestsellers 51-150* (http://www.usatoday.com/life/enter/books/leb2.htm).

*Writers and their Copyright Holders* (http://www.lib.utexas.edu/Libs/HRC/WATCH) is an invaluable resource for finding the address of those holding copyrights to various published materials. Most of these are housed in libraries and this page is targeted at scholars, but should be useful to any who seek to use quotations for their manuscripts.

## Science Fiction, Fantasy and Horror

*The Artemis Project Databook Contents* (http://www.asi.org/adb/outline.html) is a listing of working drafts on space and utilization of space that are ideal for garnering ideas.

*Australian SF Online* (http://www.asf-online.org) is a general site for Australian Science Fiction, including news, listings of writers and much much more.

*Chaos Manor Writers Research* (http://www.chaosmanor.com) is an entry point for a link to the Internet Fantasy Writers Association where you can find an excellent mailing list for those interested in writing fantasy. If you have any interest in fantasy and writing do not pass this one up.

*David Nordhaus's Crematorium* (http://www.tfs.net/nordwolc/crematorium.htm) is an interesting resource for everything to do with horror in both writing and cinema.

*Fantastic Fiction Bibliographies* (http://www.fantasticfiction.co.uk/index.html) is a compilation of over a thousand bibliographies of Science Fiction, Fantasy and Horror authors. If you seeking information on what a writer has written this might be one place to begin a search. You search either alphabetically or by keyword.

*JabberWock* (http://www.geocities.com/SunsetStrip/Lounge/2103/jabber/jabber.html) is the web site where you can find a small DOS program that generates random names of 5-8 letters in length in its default.

*Jeffrey A. Carver* (http://www.starrigger.net/advice.htp) has interesting advice available for aspiring writers.

*JMS on Writing* (http://www.geocities.com/~lunatic/jmsintro.htm) is the culled entries of J.Michael Straczynski, on writing from the usenets. This creator and writer of Babylon 5 is a truly monumental respository of wisdom on this subject and this site is well worth checking out. For those interested in science fiction and awards for the same I offer the following excellent site: SFWA Nebula Awards

*John W. Campbell Best New Writer Eligible Author Web Site* (http://www.sff.net/campbell-awards) goes a long way to providing a spot where new Science Fiction writers can showcase themselves and others can find out how to vote for these writers and the award named after this corner stone in Fannish history as far as editors and incubator for new SF talent.

*The Odyssey Summer Fantasy Writing Workshop* (http://www.sff.net/odyssey) - June 11–July 20, 2001 - Manchester, New Hampshire - Early admission starts January 31. This is an intensive experience of six weeks of fantasy, science fiction and horror writing workshop run by World Fantasy Award winning editor Jeanne Cavelos. This year's guests include Terry Bisson, Ellen Kushner, Allen Steele, and more. The site has complete info on the workshop plus writing tips, links, guest lecturer transcriptions and more.

*New Scientist.com* (http://www.newscientist.com) is a news web site for the latest in news on what is happening in science from around the world. It should provide enticing and interesting springboards for possible plot ideas for those who have a dry moment. Check it out.

*The Science Fiction Crows Nest* (http://www.sfcrowsnest.com) is a search engine, directory and general site for finding resources about science fiction whether published in novels, zines or otherwise.

*The Science Fiction and Fantasy Writers of America, Inc.* (http://www. sfwa.org) is a vital resource as an organization and equally good resource as a homepage. Among its many other resources including style guides and other resources there is the *Warnings and Cautions for Writers* (http://www.sfwa.org/Beware/Warnings.html).

*Short Fiction Roundup* (http://www.sff.net/people/jbailey/roundup) is a good resource for seeing what has been published in the science fiction magazines.

*Tangent* (http://www.sff.net/tangent) is a short fiction review magazine for Science Fiction and Fantasy and could potentially be a useful resource.

*3-D Star Maps* (http://www.clark.net/pub/nyrath/starmap.html) is an indispensible resource for all those budding star charters that would like to make their journeys to Tau Ceti and Barnard's Star accurate.

*World Building 101* (http://www.kaui.com/WB101/WB101Start.html) is just as it sounds. A short course on creating alien solar systems and an ideal resource for the speculative fiction writer.

*World Builders* (http://web.calstatela.edu/academic/builders/index. html) is along the same line as above except that this is a course being offered by the California State University at Los Angeles.

*The Worlds of Fantasy* (http://www.geocities.com/Area51/Shire/1524/index.html) is a site with a range of resources and features for the fantasy writer. It includes market reports and much more.

## Romances

*Bookbug on the Web* (http://www.geocities.com/~bookbug/home.html) describes itself as 'Resources for Romance Readers' It is that and much more, including an extensive set of links to romance writer web pages, reviews and more.

*Gothic Journal* (http://www.visi.com/romance) is one interesting place to get the pulse of the gothic romance genre.

*The Passionate Pen* (http://www.passionatepen.com) is the romance resource of an as yet unpublished romance writer. The site includes publisher guidelines and more.

*Romance Central* (http://romance-central.com) is devoted to the romance writer and provides workshops and forums to that end. If this is your genre, you might want to check here.

*Romantic Times* (http://romantictimes.com) is a great site that gives addresses of agents and publishers. It provides a wealth of information on any item involving romance novels including how to research and how to promote your writing.

*Romance Writers of America* (http://rwanational.com) provides many informational articles on writing and publishing. It also gives a list of local chapters around the U.S.

*Romance Writers Homepage* (http://www.simegen.com/out-t/romance/index.html) is described by themselves as as being a site that 'was built by romance authors for romance authors. We've listened to input, what people want, and that's what we're now aiming for. And best of all, it's totally FREE!!!' If Romance is your genre of choice, check them out and see if this is what you want.

## Mysteries

*The FBI Freedom of Information Site* (http://foia.fbi.gov) is a wealth of information about criminals and more and links to other sites of diverse content. Whether you are interested in Al Capone or fingerprinting or what have you, this is one place to possibly look.

*The Police Officer's Internet Directory* (http://www.officer.com) is a comprehensive resource of information about the Police and invaluable for those doing mysteries or police procedurals. Along with this site you might want to check out the Department of the California Highway Patrol.

*Primal Scream* (http://www.ieway.com/~csukbr) is for those into something a little on the bizarre side. It concentrates on crime and justice and facts relating to such diverse areas as serial killers and more.

## Poetry

*Alien Flower* (http://www.sonic.net/web/alienflower) describes itself as being where poets and performers have fun. It is all that and much much more.

*Comprehensive Poetry Links* (http://www.js.spokane.wa.us/poetry) has links to a variety of different sites with poetry content

*lovenpoetry.com* (http://www.lovenpoetry.com) describes itself as 'A collection of love poetry, romance poems, featured poem of the month, childrens poetry, quotes, dedications, chat, horoscopes, poetic romantic ideas, poets newsletter' It should be noted that many of the links came up as coming soon, but the site looks promising.

*Poetry Links Library* (http://www.sonic.net/layne/poetrylnk.html) has a wide range of links to resources for those interested in poetry, from markets to other.

*The Western Folklife Center's Cowboy Poet's On The Internet* (http://www.westfolk.org) includes a local group in Elko, Navada as well as live cybercasts of the poets, a Cowboy Poetry Gathering and more.

## Writing for Children

*The Children's Writing Resource Center* (http://www.write4kids.com) is presented by Children's Book Insider, a newsletter for children's writers.

*Inkspot* (http://www.inkspot.com) is an excellent resource for writers on all levels. This site has extensive resources pertaining to beginning writers, agents, writers groups and much more. Of particular interst is an area specifically designed for the Young Writer

*The Purple Crayon: A Children's Book Editor's Site* (http://www. underdown.org) is an excellent resource for those interested in writing for children. It includes articles by the author of the page as well as a wealth of links to other resources on the internet for children's writers.

*The Word Pool* (http://www.wordpool.co.uk) is a UK based resource for for parents, teachers and writers who are interested in children's books. It includes writer profiles, faqs and much more.

## Screenwriting

*The Academy of Motion Picture Arts and Science* (http://www.ampas. org) is an excellent source of information about the Academy Awards and the programs of the Academy. For those interesting in screen writing this is a useful resource. You can also pick up applications for fellowships here as well.

*Fadin* (http://home.earthlink.net/~scribbler) or the Screen Writer's Homepage is another excellent resource with late breaking news.

*The Inkwell* (http://theinkwell.com) is a writer's site with a present emphasis on screenwriters and screenwriting.

*The Internet Movie Database* (http://www.imdb.com) has a wealth of entertainment features, but its real name to fame is its extensive database of movies, TV shows, and the people who make them. If you need to do research on what has gone before, this is a very good place to start.

*Project Greenlight* (http://www.projectgreenlight.com) is actually a contest open to all amateur screenwriters. This is the brainchild of Ben Affleck and Matt Damon in association with Miramax Films and HBO. In addition to the contest itself which gives submitters the opportunity to have their screenplay produced, it is also a site with Boards, Chats and more. Check the web site out for details. So, in addition to being listed as a contest, it is also listed here as a resource.

*The Professional Screenwriters Link Page* (http://members.aol.com/linkwrite/profwrt.html) has extensive links to a variety of areas including agents.

*The Screenwriters/Playwrights Page* (http://www.teleport.com/~cdeemer/scrwriter.html) has a wealth of links and interesting tidbits about the process of screenwriting.

*Screenwriters - Producers Welcome* (http://www.insidetheweb.com/mbs.cgi/mb125238) describes itself as 'A virtual meeting place where Spec screenplay writers and Producers do lunch!' What this means is a simple, virtually graphicless message board where writers, producers and others can leave requests.

*The Screenwriters Utopia Page* (http://www.screenwritersutopia.com) is also a good resource for aspiring screenwriters and screenwriters alike.

*Screaming In the Celluloid Jungle* (http://members.tripod.com/~SiberianWolf) is an extensive site with lists of agents, resources and a range of interesting features sure to be of interest to the aspiring screenwriter.

*tvwriters.com* (http://www.tvwriter.com) is an extensive site with interesting information about screen writing and the possibility of getting your script produced. The author of the site is accepting scripts from his site for a production due out. If nothing else, check the site out for its many resources.

*The University of New Orleans DCRM Silent Movies* (http://www.uno.edu/~drcom/silents.html) web site has a wealth of links to archived quicktime movies from such masters as Charlie Chaplin, William Desmond Taylor and many many others. If you have an interest in screenwriting it is always good to know the history out of which the video explosion grew.

## Technical Writing, Journalism and Magazines

*Edit.Co.UK* (http://www.edit.co.uk) is a site for Technical Editors, Reporters and those who want to reach them.

*Gary Conroy's Technical Writing* (http://techwriting.miningco.com) page is an interesting resource of information about this lucrative area.

*The Health Law Resource* (http://www.netreach.net/~wmanning) is a useful source if medical legal information is pertinent to what you are writing.

*The Magazine and Newsletter Editor's Resource List* (http://www.tfs.net/personal/tgoff/erlist.html) has a wealth of links for everything from professional cartoonists, Pulitzer Prizes and much more.

*Technical Writing: Books and Reference Sources* (http://www.interlog.com/~ksoltys/twritres.html) is an exhaustive bibliography divided into a multiplicity of areas of interest to technical writers.

## Dictionaries and Word References

*Altavista's Babelfish* (http://babelfish.altavista.digital.com) site provides the opportunity to translate from one language to another. This is not perfect, but might give some beginning options. If nothing else it can be a hilarious exercise to translate from one language to another and back to the original again and see the results.

*Bucknell University's Online Grammar* (http://www.bucknell.edu/~rbeard/grammars.html) explores an entirely different area. Here you can find the grammars for a variety of languages including Akkadina, Bengali and Cree to name only a few.

*Damon Knight's Discussion of Plot* (http://www.efn.org/~dknight) is an excerpt from Creating Short Fiction and is an excellent account of this often difficult component of writing.

William Strunk's classic **Elements of Style** (http://www.columbia.edu/acis/bartleby/strunk) as well as John Bartlett's also classic Familiar Quotations are both available on the Web thanks to Columbia University's Project Bartleby.

*Garbl's Writing Resources On-Line* (http://garbl.home.comcast.net) is a quite useful compendium of 'English language, grammar, style, writing, usage' and much more. Well worth a look.

*Grammar and Style Notes* (http://www.english.upenn.edu/~jlynch/Grammar) is an interesting and useful reference whose author admits happily that his rules are not set in stone.

*Helpful Addresses: 9000+ Public Libraries and Their Links* (http://www.acclaimed.com/helpful/lib-add.htm) is a particularly interesting resource for research and also has links to similar resources for newspapers.

*The Human-Languages Page* (http://www.june29.com/HLP) catalogs the resources for linguistic study and learning on the web

*The Internet Speculative Fiction Database* (http://www.cu-online.com/~avonruff/sfdbase.html) is the place to go to research on awards, forthcoming books and much more.

In the category of reference homepages you can explore in the **Marriam Webster Language Center** (http://www.m-w.com) that links to a variety of resources including the **Webster Dictionary, the American English Dictionary and Roget's Thesaurus on line and a List of Dictionaries** (http://math-www.uni-paderborn.de/HTML/Dictionaries.html) where you'll find German to English dictionaries and much more. You can download and view detailed maps from around the world thanks to the **PCL Map Collection** (http://www.lib.utexas.edu/Libs/PCL/Map_collection/Map_collection.html). Also useful are the links of interest that can be found at the homepage for ***On-Line Literary Research Tools*** (http://www.english.upenn.edu/~jlynch/Lit).

***OneLook Dictionaries*** (http://www.onelook.com) is a central site for exploring words in a variety of languages via an interface that links you with a variety of dictionaries throughout the internet. Well worth a visit.

***The On-Line English Grammar*** (http://www.edunet.com/english/ grammar/index.html) is an interesting site to discover everything you ever wanted to know about the structure of the language we use as writers.

***Plumb Design Visual Thesaurus*** (http://www.plumbdesign.com/ thesaurus) is a visual experience of language of a kind unique and open to a host of serendipitous discoveries that cannot be charted easily. Check the instructions and wait for it to load. It is indeed well worth the wait.

***The University of Virginia Electronic Text Library*** (http://etext.lib. virginia.edu/uvaonline.html) is a good resource that provides texts of a variety of kind in English, German, French, Japanese and Latin.

A Web of On-Line Dictionaries (http://www.bucknell.edu/~rbeard/ diction.html) is just as it sounds, a massive collection of links to all manner of dictionaries. This includes links to language dictionaries that range from Afrikaans to Xhosa and even an area for Language Identifiers and Guessers.

***The Wordbot*** (http://www.cs.washington.edu/homes/kgolden/wordbot. html) appears to provide a variety of dictionaries and the ability to translate from one language to another.

***Word A Day*** (http://www.wordsmith.org/awad) is a mailing list that emails out a vocabulary word a day with definition and sometimes commentary.

***The Writers Free Reference*** (http://www.writers-free-reference.com) is a quick list of links to everything from mailing addresses for non-fee agents to lyrics of songs and much more.

# *Read More*

## Recently released titles
## from the Author

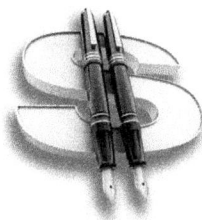

## Media Tipping Points

By Dr. Philip Gordon, PhD

Tipping Points as evidenced in global events are, in many ways, influenced by media. This insightful book by Dr. Philip Gordon, PhD, details three case studies which were selected on the basis of common Tipping Point attributes: they each involved media contagiousness and stickiness during their development, and, each arrived at a moment in time, which could be characterized by the phenomenon of Tipping Points.

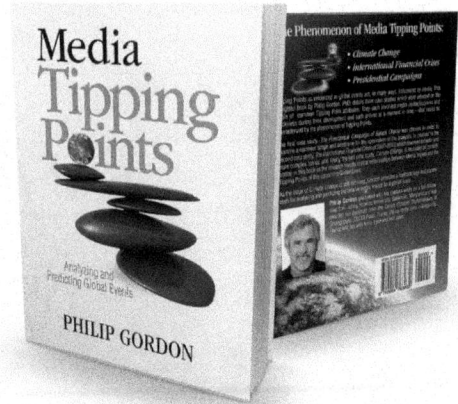

The first case study, the Presidential Campaign of Barack Obama was chosen in order to examine a narrower scope and timeframe for the application of the analysis, in contrast to the second case study, the International Financial Crisis of 2007-2010, which involved broader and more complex issues, and finally, the last case study, Climate Change, is included as consideration in this book as the research reveals critical relationships between Media Impact and the Tipping Points of this upcoming Global Event.

As the issue of Climate Change is still evolving, Gordon provides a methodology and parameters for analyzing and predicting the relative media impact on a global scale.

On Amazon.com now!
http://www.amazon.com/Media-Tipping-Points-Analyzing-Predicting/dp/098476383X/

(Coming soon in eBook version on Smashwords.com)

# Principles and Practices of Lighting Design:
## The Art of Lighting Composition

By Dr. Philip Gordon,
PhD, LC, NCQLD

A complete handbook on
Lighting Design with both
Artistic and Technical
approaches for the beginning to
advanced lighting designer.

Dr. Philip Gordon, PhD, LC,
NCQLD has written a "must
have" handbook that includes
applications and case studies as well
as updated product advances, specifications, resources and guides.
Suitable for educational programs, professionals and related design
fields. Also includes theory and resources for individuals interested
in the future of the lighting design profession. Philip has combined
several types of lighting books (theory, application, case study and
resource) into one volume. A perfect resource for any design reference.

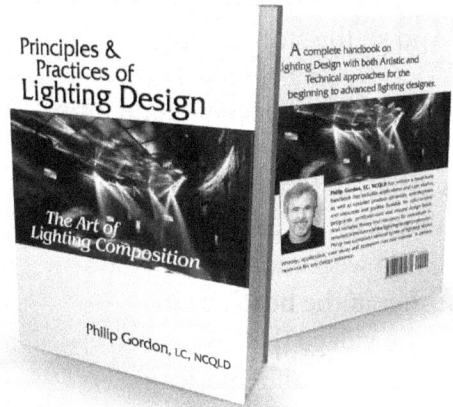

On Amazon.com now!
http://www.amazon.com/Principles-Practices-Lighting-Design-
Composition/dp/0615471633/

(also in eBook version on Smashwords.com)

## Journey To Burgundy: Secrets d'Histoire

By Dr. Philip Gordon, PhD

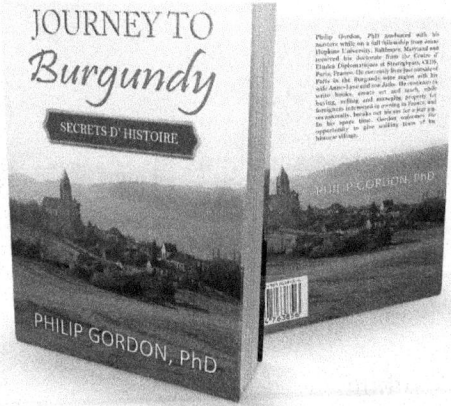

And so the story starts…

AL and I had become fond of traveling around the different villages of France, as it was always an excuse for us to spend weekends and holidays either at the beach or in some village that I've never seen, being an American from California. And so, when we moved to Burgundy France, about an hour southeast of Paris, it seemed like a very good solution and to start thinking about a life together…

On Amazon.com now!
http://www.amazon.com/Journey-Burgundy-dHistoire-Philip-Gordon/dp/0984763856

## The Zodiac Project

By Dr. Philip Gordon, PhD

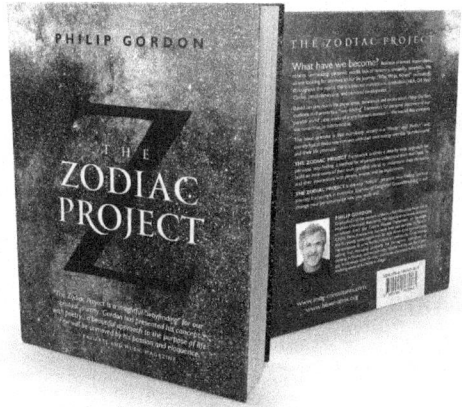

"The Zodiac Project is a insightful, "wayfinding" technique for understanding our spiritual energy journey. Dr. Gordon presents his concept with poetry... a beautiful approach to the meaning and purpose of life. Few will be unmoved by his passion and eloquence".

On Amazon.com now!
http://www.amazon.com/Zodiac-Project-Philip-Gordon/dp/0984763864/

## Pendulum

By Dr. Philip Gordon, PhD

If you could change one thing about yourself, what would it be?

Renew my body, set at 17.

-Allen Ginsberg

1988, Chicago:

Stare deeply into the watery blue eyes of an elderly and
wheelchair bound man, pull back and you'll find yourself surrounded by the serenity of the manicured lawn of the Thousand Oaks Convalescent Hospital… his home for the past 30 years.

Physical examinations must be done periodically, as with all of the elderly. For David Jason, it's an opportunity to briefly escape the confines of this limited world.  Today's ambulance ride with his nurse and confidant, Angela Ryan, to Lakeview General Hospital will be unlike any other;… it will alter his life forever… embarking on mankind's most impossible dream… a second.chance… to go through life again knowing what he knows now.

On the way to the hospital there is a terrible accident, a collision between the ambulance and a careening eighteen wheeler out of control! Angela is thrown clear, and David a concussion and deep lacerations; he is fortunate. Tests are done, and their conclusions are shocking.  It seems as though David's cells are multiplying at an alarming rate, reversing metabolically to such an extent that he is actually regressing in age!  He may only have 6 months to live, as the physiological trauma of the regeneration process is determined to be too much for his life support systems.

On Amazon.com now!
http://www.amazon.com/Pendulum-Original-Screenplay-Philip-Gordon/dp/1477487336/

(also in eBook version on Smashwords.com)

# Philip "Flip" Gordon: Jazz Compositions: Volume 1

By Dr. Philip "Flip" Gordon, PhD

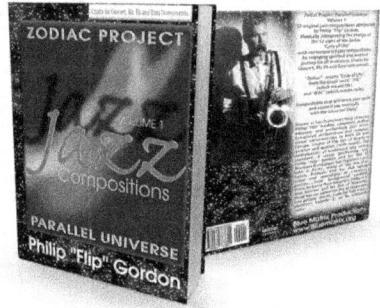

The Zodiac Project: Parallel Universe: Philip "Flip" Gordon : Jazz Compositions: Volume 1: The Zodiac Project: Parallel Universe: Consists of 12 contemporary jazz compositions which musically interpret the energy and journey of the 12 Zodiac Signs, i.e. an avant-garde, spiritual and metaphysical "cycle of life" Jazz Charts for: Concert, B♭, E♭ and Bass Instrumentation. Written and performed in Paris, France.

For PRINT ordering information, please visit: http://www.amazon.com/Philip-Flip-Gordon-Compositions-Parrallel/dp/0984763805

For EBOOK ordering information, please visit: http://www.smashwords.com/books/view/135942

12 original jazz compositions composed by Philip "Flip" Gordon. Musically interpreting the energy of the 12 signs of the Zodiac "Cycle of Life" with contemporary jazz compositions. An engaging spiritual and musical journey for all musicians. Charts for Concert, B♭, E♭ and Bass instruments.

- "Zodiac" - means "Cycle of Life", from the Greek word: "ZOE" (which means life), and "DIAC" (which means cycle)

Compositions that will move your spirit and connect you musically with the universe! Enjoy!

Known as San Francisco's King of Swing, Philip "Flip" Gordon: composer, author, educator and performing jazz artist. Completed performance and compositional conservatories in both US and Europe. Leader of The Out of Nowhere quartet and quintet (with vocals), the ambassadors of traditional jazz swing standard. A classy performing act, Philip "Flip" Gordon and his Out of Nowhere Band plays San Francisco (and now in Paris), many of the five-star hotels, festivals and the club swing scene and specializes in corporate parties... from background cocktail music to dance floor favorites. Philip is a true crooner and his Out of Nowhere Band has an extensive list of corporate and private clients. Look for Jazz Compositions: Volume 2!

## Philip "Flip" Gordon: Jazz Compositions: Volume 2

By Dr. Philip "Flip" Gordon, PhD

The Zodiac Project: Secrets d'Histoire: Philip "Flip" Gordon: Jazz Compositions Volume 2: Zodiac Project: Secrets D'Histoire: 12 original jazz compositions composed by Philip "Flip" Gordon. An engaging jazz musical journey for all musicians. Charts for Concert, B♭, E♭ and Bass Instrumentation.

For PRINT ordering information, please visit: http://www.amazon.com/Philip-Flip-Gordon-Jazz-Compositions/dp/0984763899

For EBOOK ordering information, please visit: http://www.smashwords.com/books/view/65358

12 original jazz compositions composed by Philip "Flip" Gordon. Musically interpreting the energy of the 12 signs of the Zodiac "Cycle of Life" with contemporary jazz compositions. An engaging spiritual and musical journey for all musicians. Charts for Concert, B♭, E♭ and Bass instruments.

- "Zodiac" - means "Cycle of Life", from the Greek word: "ZOE" (which means life), and "DIAC" (which means cycle)

Compositions that will move your spirit and connect you musically with the universe! Enjoy!

Known as San Francisco's King of Swing, Philip "Flip" Gordon: composer, author, educator and performing jazz artist. Completed performance and compositional conservatories in both US and Europe. Leader of The Out of Nowhere quartet and quintet (with vocals), the ambassadors of traditional jazz swing standard. A classy performing act, Philip "Flip" Gordon and his Out of Nowhere Band plays San Francisco (and now in Paris), many of the five-star hotels, festivals and the club swing scene and specializes in corporate parties... from background cocktail music to dance floor favorites. Philip is a true crooner and his Out of Nowhere Band has an extensive list of corporate and private clients. Volume 3: to be released soon!

## Philip Gordon: Reflections

By Dr. Philip Gordon, PhD

Selected poems and photography written and compiled by the artist during his life journey growing up on the east coast (Jersey and Washington DC), after graduate school, Johns Hopkins University, moving to San Francisco and Palo Alto, California, then off to jazz and classical music conservatories and PhD in Paris, France followed by a blissful retirement with his wife and sons.

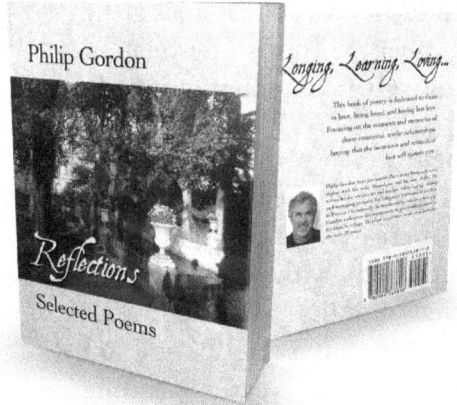

For PRINT ordering information, please visit:
http://www.amazon.com/Philip-Gordon-Reflections-Selected-Poems/dp/0984763813

For EBOOK ordering information, please visit:
https://www.smashwords.com/books/view/139594

**And Coming Soon!**
On Amazon.com and Smashwords.com:

## Insider's Guide: Paris Hotel Market

Worldwide visitors: France is the Number 1 Tourist destination again: Over 74 million visitors!

There were 74 million visits to Paris by overseas residents – an increase of 4 per cent when compared with the previous three months, and up 5 per cent on the same period on the previous year. Spending decreased by 2 per cent compared to the previous 3 months, but showed an increase of 8 per cent with the same period a year earlier.

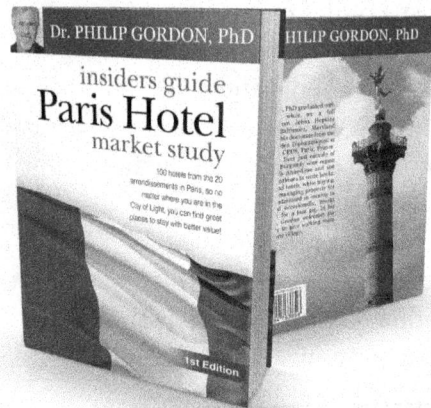

Visits overseas by Paris residents decreased by 4 per cent (to 16.7 million) when compared with the previous three months, but again showed an increase of 2 per cent when compared with the same period a year earlier. Spending decreased by 1 per cent compared to the previous 3 months, but showed an increase of 6 per cent within the same period a year earlier.

Visits by overseas residents to Paris rose by 6 per cent during the last 12 months. The number of visits from residents of North America showed an increase of 4 per cent (to 4.4 million), from residents of Western Europe of 5 per cent (to 20.0 million), and from other parts of the world of 10 per cent (to 6.8 million).

The increase in tourism and increase for business bookings bodes well for the immediate future.

This upcoming Blue Matrix Publication presents an up-to-date, fact filled, insiders' guide to the The Paris Hotel Market:

Numbers of Hotels by Category, Numbers of rooms, and Occupancy Rates and Periods, Occupancy Locations (Paris wide) and Typical Room Prices.

## Charles Baudelaire: Life in Paris:

By Dr. Philip Gordon, PhD

This upcoming Blue Matrix Publications book will focus on the chronology and geographical life of Charles Baudelaire. A journey through Paris during his lifetime and the particular effect these important Parisian places and events had on this writer's life and work. Naturally, this journey will inevitably include references to the many with numerous influential artists of that era as well as the locations where these events occurred. And, as we will discover, Baudelaire drew many others into his orbit as he had a variety of significant exchanges during his life there.

Excerpts of his actual writings and prose are included in the chapters that follow, to draw parallels and perhaps illustrate what Baudelaire was experiencing in Paris during this time in history and his life. Each chapter will include a locator map and outline the relevance of the various sites to his life journey.

The Paris during the era that Baudelaire lived and wrote certainly influenced his art. But the city of Paris did more than color his mood or direct his attention to the selection of detail or subjects for his work. In many instances, Paris and the people, and his feelings towards them, became his subject matter. Here presented in this book, is the cityscape of Paris then and now, with the precise identification of the places he worked, lived, played, rested, drank and ultimately influenced this literary legend.

The beginning for our journey about his life in Paris will be centered around his masterpiece, Les Fleurs du Mal which was constructed in such a way that the dialogue between the poet and his public life in Paris inevitably degenerates into an unequal duel, and leads to the impression that the space of art and the space of bourgeois Paris society are and have been from the beginning incapable of coming together. Baudelaire, feeling the angst of his own life, is the intruder in the bourgeois in this social space, i.e. Baudelaire is the outcast, and inevitably the scapegoat, accepting of his role as the victim and the accuser. Baudelaire made it very clear he was not one to tolerate the rules of the rich. Anything that created a metaphor for the poverty of the soul and exposes those who do not know anything about the phenomenon of poverty and social injustice were in his sights.

When the court banned the six poems in Les Fleurs du Mal, the poetic journey, or, secret architecture that Baudelaire had created with this collection of prose, were significantly altered. The three primary themes; the voyage from birth, art and love (life in the city, stimulants, perversion and rebellion) and finally death, are in total, a means by which the reader is invited to share the real life journey of Charles Baudelaire.

In Les Fleurs du Mal, Baudelaire wrote:

*Today, the Poet, when he would conceive*
*These native grandeurs, where now can be seen*
*Women and men in all their nakedness,*
*Feels in his soul a chill of hopelessness*
*Before this miserable and bleak tableau.*
*Monstrosities that cry to be clothed!*
*Bodies grotesque and only fit for masques!*
*Poor twisted trunks, scrawny and gone to flab,*
*Whose god, implacable Utility,*
*In brazen wraps, swaddles his progeny!*

No writer's life illustrates the meaning of painful irony more than the Charles Baudelaire. Endowed with a natural gift for writing, and blessed with having come from a wealthy family constitution, this poet was at the same time a genius of self-delusion, and a craftsman of his own miserable existence. Reading his poetry is an ordeal, as it becomes very clear that he was self-destructive and had placed himself again and again in situations, which, only, in turn, bore their evidence in his literary works. The obsessive regularity that Baudelaire created during his life in Paris, that he constantly craved to escape, leads one to ask the question:

Did this despair belong to the very essence of his creative drive?

*And he went home alone... he said to himself: 'Today I have had in my imagination, three homes; each has given me equal pleasure. Why force my body to move from place to place, since my soul can travel so nimbly? And why in turn plan into reality, when the plan is in itself such sufficient pleasure?'*

*- Les Fenetres*

## Other Titles:

On Amazon.com and Smashwords.com:

- **Chasing the Carrot: Volume 1: The Story**
  By Dr. Philip Gordon, PhD

The year was 2000, the Dotcom "Bubble" had yet to burst, opportunity seemed possible everywhere, it all started with an idea...

- **Chasing the Carrot: Volume 2: The Mission**
  By Dr. Philip Gordon, PhD

The detailed Business Plan, Market Analysis, Forecast of Revenue, Potential Users and Rewards... the complete A-Z volume of launching one of the most innovative and socially responsible websites prior to the dot com bubble bursting. A valuable resource for entrepreneurial endeavors for those individuals and entities who choose to think and act out of the box.

This Volume 2 complements: Chasing the Carrot: Volume 1: My Story